MOSES

PRINCE OF EGYPT~ SON OF ABRAHAM

Printed in the United States of America.
Second printing.

THIS WORK IS A PRODUCT of:

Ken Bangs Writing

I0836440

Moses: Prince of Egypt ~ Son of Abraham is composed in cambria and edited by Grammarly Professional.

Cover Photo Credit: Unedited image of Moses With the Ten Commandments by Otto Semler based on the engravings by Carolsfeld, in the public domain.

Baby Moses Found by Pharaoh's Daughter
Exodus 2:3-6

Illustrations from old Bible story books,
coutesy of La Vista Church of Christ. Public Domain.
http://lavistachurchofchrist.org/Pictures/Moses%20to%20the%20Judges/target1.html

Moses was Egyptian Royalty by decree of Pharaoh Seti; but he was Hebrew and heir to the Abramhamic Covenant by birth.

Prelude

MOSES: Prince of Egypt ~ Son of Abraham is a novel. I have not written it as a historical study or treatise on Moses. My intention is to entertain while offering the reader a different perspective of Moses and the events that impacted his legacy.

In the Prelude, I will introduce the reader to the principal characters and the different people groups, the resources used in researching the life story of one of the most complicated men in the history of our world, and then present some ancillary information intended to bridge the gap between reality and legend; for the legacy of Moses is comprised of both. To fully follow the story, one must be able and willing to blend the two.

INTRODUCTION
RESEARCH RESOURCES~

Wikipedia ~Wikipedia describes itself as "an online free-content encyclopedia project helping create a world in which everyone can freely share in the sum of all knowledge. It is supported by the Wikimedia Foundation and is based on a model of freely editable content. The name "Wikipedia" is a combination of the words wiki (a technology for creating collaborative websites, from the Hawaiian word wiki, meaning "quick") and Encyclopedia. Wikipedia's articles provide links designed to guide the user to related pages with additional information."

The Jewish Encyclopedia ~ The Jewish Encyclopedia: is an English-language presentation containing over 15,000 articles on the history, culture, and state of Judaism from the earliest days up to the early 20th century.

It was initially published in 12 volumes between 1901 and 1906 by Funk & Wagnalls of New York and reprinted in the 1960s by KTAV Publishing House. The Encyclopedia's managing editor was Isidore Singer, and the editorial board was chaired by Isaac K. Funk and Frank H. Vizetelly.

The work's scholarship is still highly regarded. The American Jewish Archives deemed it "the most monumental Jewish scientific work of modern times." Rabbi Joshua L. Segal said, "for events before 1900; it is considered to offer a level of scholarship superior to either of the more recent Jewish encyclopedias written in English."

It is now in the public domain.

Antiquities of the Jews ~

This is a 20-volume historiographical work, written in Greek, by the Jewish historian Flavius Josephus in the 13th year of the reign of Roman emperor Flavius Domitian which was around A.D. 93 or 94.

Antiquities of the Jews contains an account of the history of the Jewish people for *Josephus' gentile patrons.* Some question the authenticity of much of his work, suspecting that the Romans employed him to complete the works casting them in the most possible favorable light. In the first ten volumes, Josephus follows the events of the historical books of the Hebrew Bible, beginning with the creation of Adam and Eve.

The second ten volumes continue the history of the Jewish people beyond the biblical text and up to the Jewish War, or the First Jewish–Roman War, 66 to 73 C.E. This work, along with Josephus's other major work, The Jewish War (De Bello Iudaico), provides valuable background material for historians wishing to understand 1st-century A.D. Judaism and the early Christian period.

The Scripture ~

a collection of religious texts, writings, or scriptures sacred in Judaism and Christianity. It appears in the form of an anthology, a compilation of texts of various forms linked by the belief that they are collectively revelations of God.

These texts include theologically focused historical accounts, hymns, prayers, proverbs, parables, didactic letters, admonitions, essays, poetry, and prophecies. Believers also generally consider the Bible to be a product of divine inspiration.

Principal People Groups ~

The Hebrews ~
The origin of the term Hebrew – and the history of the enslavement of the people

Wikipedia identifies the book of Genesis as the first book of the Hebrew Bible and the Christian Old Testament. It describes the book as an account of the world's creation, the early history of humanity, Israel's ancestors, and the origins of the Hebrew people. Its' Hebrew name is the same as its' first word, Bereshis (בהתחלה) meaning, in the beginning.

The second book of Moses, Exodus (Shemot in Hebrew). Exodus means going out, migration or immigration and is usually used when discussing a large group of people.

In the book of Genesis, chapter 15: 12-16 (NKJ), we read, "Now when the sun was going down, a deep sleep fell upon Abram, and behold horror and great darkness fell upon him. Then He told Abram: Know that your descendants will be strangers in a land that is not theirs and will serve them, and they will afflict them four hundred years. And also, the nation whom they serve, I will judge, afterward they shall come out with great possessions.... but in the fourth generation they shall return here..."

Thus, is given the prophecy in which the EXODUS, described in the second book of Moses, is seeded. Or is it?

At first reading, our mind races forward to what we know of biblical history; we know His people were strangers in Egypt, that they were afflicted by the Egyptians, and left taking great possessions with them.

We think God was referring to Egypt and the Egyptians' land when he spoke of those whom His people will serve and be afflicted by. If so, then what did he mean by saying, "Also I give to you and your descendants, after you, the land in which you are a stranger, all the land of Canaan... (Genesis 17:8)."

The answer lies in the last sentence of the former verses quoted, "but in the fourth generation, they shall *return here.*" By this, we know that Abram was in Canaan when given the prophecy in a dream.

So, how did it happen, how did the enslavement of the Hebrews begin?

Let's start with this poem by the author...

Down from the north with a great army, he swept, Penetrated the country, then turned left.

East to Jerusalem, Nebuchadnezzar set course. The holy city could surrender or fall by force.

They rejected his demand and closed the gates. The great King was patient, choosing to wait.

Then he struck with violence and rage,
He Burned the gates, the walls razed

He conquered and pillaged with a relentless hand. The brightest young nobles took to his land.

These opening lines of Captivities' Freedom give us a picture of how the people who became known as Hebrews were enslaved and transported to their conquerors' land to serve.

Captivities' Freedom is about the enslavement of Daniel by Nebuchadnezzar, the great King of the North, who was the ruler of ancient Babylon.

But history suggests that the Hebrews were also taken in slavery to foreign lands to serve their captors long before this.

In 722 BCE, the Assyrians under Sargon II captured the Kingdom of Israel and transported the young nobles to Mesopotamia. Then came Nebuchadnezzar, who captured Jerusalem and transported more to Babylon.

The captives proved to be a hardy and industrious lot. Their captors used them to build infrastructure, manage the finances, and to operate the government.

Then we read the account of Joseph being sold into slavery by his jealous brothers. He eventually became the slave of Potifar. He is introduced to the Pharaoh, gains favor, and is appointed vizier of Egypt.

This would mean that Moses' ancestors had been enslaved in Egypt long before his birth. But it was during Joseph's service as vizir that the people began to increase exponentially, to prosper in captivity, and to gain the reputation for ingenuity and industry that caused the pharaohs to both value and fear them as a people. Some suggest that it was also during this time that they became known as Hebrews.

To say that history, how these people became known as Hebrews is not clear would be an understatement.

But this we know; the Word Hebrew is first seen in Genesis 14:13 when Abram is referred to as "the Hebrew."

The editors of the Spirit-Filled life bible, ©1982 Thomas Nelson, Inc., notes that in this verse, the term Hebrew is tied to Eber (see Genesis 10:25), whose name means to pass through or to describe one who is descended from or is of Eber.

Strong's supports the definition of one who passes over or traverses; The Biblical term Ivri (עברי; Hebrew pronunciation: [ʕivˈri]), meaning "to traverse" or "to pass over," is usually rendered as Hebrew in English, from the ancient Greek Ἑβραῖος and the Latin Hebraeus.

Strong's suggests Hebrew written as עבר (ever, Strong's #5677) and is derived from the verb עבר (Ah. B.R., Strong's 5674), which means "to cross over" or "to pass through."

The noun derived from this verb is עבר (ever, Strong's #5676) and means "the other side," which is also the meaning of the name Eber. The Word Eber appears first in Genesis 10:25.

This is an interesting play on words, especially when considering that as a baby, Moses passed from his Hebrew birth to his Egyptian raising by floating on/over or through and was drawn from the river Nile. And that the Hebrews passed through the Red Sea and crossed over the Jordan to gain their place in the promised land.

The combination of the two cultures is seen in his name. His name was From the Hebrew הֶשֹׁמ (Mosheh), which is most likely derived from Egyptian meaning "son," but could also possibly mean "deliver" in Hebrew.

The definition suggested in the Old Testament of "drew out" from Hebrew משה (mashah) is probably an invented etymology (see Exodus 2:10).

The origin of the Midianites

According to the Book of Genesis, the Midianites were the descendants of Midian, who was a son of Abraham and his wife Keturah: "Abraham took a wife, and her name was Keturah. And she bares him Zimran, and Jokshan, and Medan, and Midian, and Ishbak, and Shuah" (Genesis 25:1–2, King James Version).

The Origin of the Cush (Kush)

The Cush came from a region known as Lower Nubia and later of the Nubian kingdom at Napata, known as the Kingdom of Kush. Kush stretched from the Upper Nile to the Red Sea.

The Origin of the Ethiopians

According to Wikipedia; The Solomonic dynasty (Amharic: ሰሎሞናዊው ሥርወ መንግሥት Sälomonawīwi širiwä menigišiti), also known as the House of Solomon, whose members claim lineal descent from the biblical King Solomon and the Queen of Sheba. Tradition asserts that the Queen gave birth to Menelik I, after her biblically described visit to Solomon in Jerusalem. In 1270, the Zagwe dynasty of Ethiopia was overthrown by Yekuno Amlak, who claimed descent from Solomon and founded the Solomonic era of Ethiopia. The dynasty lasted until 1974, when it was ended by a coup d'état and the deposition of Haile Selassie, who was a Solomonic prince through his grandmother.

The Druze

There are thought to be around 1 million Druze people in the world today; their secretive religion is believed by historians to have been developed as a movement within Islam. While the spiritual elements of their religion are highly guarded and known only to the elders, the known practices are made up of various religions, including Hinduism, Christianity, Islam, and Judaism. This variety is most likely based on historical gatherings that are typical of nomadic people.

Therefore, it is doubtful that Moses' father-in-law, Jethro, could have been a Druze priest because the Biblical Jethro lived about 1400 BCE, being somewhat older than Moses. That date greatly predates the founding of Islam-related religions by thousands of years.

But it is generally agreed that Jethro was a priest of Midian. So, who did the midinettes worship? History shows that they had both a religious and political connection with the Moabites, who worshipped a multitude of gods, including Baal-Peor and the Queen of Heaven, Ashteroth.

But, In the Book of Exodus, we see that Jethro became a worshiper of Yahweh. Chapter 18, verses 10 tells us that Jethro visited with Moses at the mountain of God. After hearing all that the Lord had done in delivering the Hebrews from Pharoah and in sustaining them in the wilderness, Jethro declared, "B*lessed be the Lord, who has delivered you out of the hand of the Egyptians and out of the hand of Pharaoh, and who has delivered the people from under the hand of the Egyptians."* He continued in verse 11; *Now I know that the Lord is greater than all the gods...* In verse 12, "Jethro took a burnt offering and other sacrifices to offer to Yahweh.

This novel references the historical blending of Ethiopians, Midianites, and the Cush peoples. To take the story forward without interrupting the flow, the reader must know that Wikipedia quotes the Jewish historian about these peoples: "Josephus gives an account of the nation of Cush, who was the son of Ham and grandson of Noah: For of the four sons of Ham, the time has not at all hurt the name of Cush; for the Ethiopians, over whom he reigned, are even at this day, both by themselves and by all men in Asia, called Cushites" (Antiquities of the Jews 1.6).

Consider this in support of that quote; The Book of Numbers 12:1 calls a wife of Moses "a Cushite woman," whereas Moses's wife Zipporah is usually described as hailing from Midian. Are these references of the same woman or were there two?

Principal Characters~

Levi was one of the twelve sons of Jacob. He became the Patriarch of the tribe of Levi, a group of clans of religious functionaries in ancient Israel who were given a special religious status (Levites), conjecturally for slaughtering idolaters of the golden calf during the time of Moses (Ex. 32:25–29). The levities had religious and political duties in the nation of Israel after Joshua led the Jews into their promised land. All the tribes, save the Levites, were given land. The Levites were given cities but were not allowed to be landowners because "the Lord God of Israel is their inheritance," as Joshua said to them" (Joshua 13:33).

In return, the landed tribes were expected to give tithes to the Levities (known as the Kohanim), working as priests in the Temple in Jerusalem, particularly the tithe known as the Maaser Rishon. The Levites who were not working as Kohanim played music in the Temple or served as guards.

Amram, an enslaved Hebrew from the tribe of Levi, the father of Moses.

Jochabed, an enslaved Hebrew also from the tribe of Levi, wife of Amram, and the mother of Moses.

Moses (1391–1271 BCE), the son of Amram and Jochabed, a descendant of Jacob of the tribe of Levi, was born into slavery, rescued from death, and adopted into the Egyptian royal family, but nourished by the milk of his Hebrew ancestry; declared by royal decree to be a Prince of Egypt, but destined to lead his people from captivity in the fulfillment of the promise made to his people by Abraham.

Wikipedia declares Moses, also known as Moshe Rabbenu (Hebrew: וְנִבַּר הַשֵּׁם lit. "Moshe, our Teacher, was the most important prophet in Judaism, and an important prophet in Christianity, Islam, the Bahá'í Faith, and several other

Abrahamic religions. In the biblical and Qur'anic (relating to or contained in the Koran) narrative, he was the leader of the Israelites and lawgiver to whom the authorship of the Torah (the first five books of the Bible) is attributed.

It is important to note that not all historians believe that Moses was a historical person. Some believe he was a legend created by oppressed people to help them deal with their captivity and enslavement.

Dr. William Guinn Dever, Distinguished Professor of the History of Israel and Near Eastern Archaeology, has written, "Legend has it that a Moses-like figure existed in the Southern Transjordan, but Egyptian historical documents and artifacts from archeological sites contain no evidence such a man lived." Dr. Dever refers to the absence of documents or other data, or materials in the many tombs opened, particularly in the Valley of the Kings.

On the other hand, those who support Moses as a historical personage point out that numerous mentions of Moses are found in the writings of Josephus.

Josephus used transcripts taken from the Temple after the Romans destroyed it in 70 A.D. to write about the enslavement of the Jews by the Egyptians. He notes that while the Egyptians relished the prosperity they enjoyed from the ingenuity of the enslaved Jews, they became concerned over the increase of the Jewish population. They feared the Jews would rebel or join with their enemies, especially the Ethiopians and the Midianites, against Pharaoh.

Seti, the Pharoah of Egypt at the time of Moses' birth. Seti was the son of Pharoah Ramses and the father of Ramses II (also known as Ramses the Great).

Moses is reported to have been born in the period between February and April 1391 B.C. Shortly before his birth, Seti had dreamed that his kingdom would be lost in a rebellion.

He went to his astrologers asking for an interpretation of the dream; they warned him that the stars indicated the Hebrews he held in captivity were plotting a rebellion. That rebellion would be led by a baby not yet born but who, when grown, was destined to deliver the Hebrews from captivity.

Fearing the loss of his kingdom, Seti issued a royal command that every male Hebrew newborn should be killed.

During this attempt to control the population growth, Moses is born and set adrift on the river Nile where he is rescued and adopted by Pharaoh's daughter.

Ramses II, the son of Pharoah Seti, the grandson of Pharoah Ramses. He was destined to follow his father as Pharoah.

Hatshepsut, An Egyptian princess, the daughter of Seti, she drew Moses from the Nile and raised him as her son. Hatsheput served in her father's court as Queen after her mother died. Seti did not want to remarry and named his daughter to serve in the largely ceremonial role as Queen, but He also named her an officer in the Egyptian Army. In naming a woman to be an officer in the Army, he broke with the tradition of appointing only males to the command ranks; and this break proved pivotal in the training of Moses as a leader of the Hebrew nation.

We do not know when Hatsheput was born, but we do know that she began her rule as Queen in 1512 B.C.

That would mean that she was not yet Queen when she rescued Moses from the Nile. Exodus 2:10 refers to her simply as Pharoah's daughter.

She ruled for twenty -two years. Her reign is known as one of the most successful in Egyptian history. She had great favor with her father, not so much so with her brother Ramses, II.

Moses was an overachiever as a child, and Seti doted on him. Ramses II was jealous of Moses and constantly pointed out that Moses was a Hebrew with no royal lineage and would never ascend to the throne.

Moses would not have had the advantages, education, military training afforded the children of royalty without the Queen's influence with her father, the Pharoah, and without her being an officer in the Egyptian Army.

The education and militaristic training are evident in the shaping of Moses into the influential leader of the Hebrew nation that history shows him to have been.

Hatshepsut's died in 1458 B.C. Archaeological excavations of her sarcophagus, found in the 20th tomb of the Valley of the Kings (KV20), we know that she probably died of a combination of diabetes, bone cancer, and an infection from an abscessed tooth. Moses more than likely did not see her while he was in exile for 40 years in the desert." But Josephus writes that artifacts, jewelry, and notes found in her sarcophagus indicate that she became a believer in the Jewish God, before her death, primarily because of the power she saw in the miracles, and plagues. Finally, the parting of the sea of reeds (red sea) as the Hebrews fled from the Egyptian Army. This has not been confirmed by any secular historian.

Miriam, biological sister of Moses.

Aaron, biological brother of Moses.

Jethro, also known as Ruel, a high priest of the Druze in Midian, father of Zipporah who became Moses' wife during his forty years in the backside of the desert.

Zipporah, an Ethiopian daughter of Jethro, who became the wife of Moses.

Montu, also spelled Mont, Monthu, or Mentu, in ancient Egyptian religion, god of the 4th Upper Egyptian nome (province), whose original capital of Hermonthis (present-day Armant) was replaced by Thebes during the 11th dynasty (2081–1939 bce). Montu was a god of war.

Relevant Locations

<u>Goshen</u>, also known as the Land of Goshen. Goshen was in lower ancient Egypt. Moses was born and raised in Goshen.

<u>Midian</u>, a desert region in the Sinai desert. Moses fled to Midian after he murdered the Egyptian who he found beating a Hebrew.

Mt. Nebo and Pisgah

'Then Moses went up from the plains of Moab to Mount Nebo, to the top of Pisgah, which is across from Jericho. And the Lord showed him all the land of Gilead as far as Dan... Then the Lord said to him, this is the land of which I swore to give Abraham, Isaac, and Jacob, saying I will give it to your descendants. I have caused you to see it with your eyes, but you shall not cross over there." (Deuteronomy 34:1-4 NKJ)

If Moses climbed Mount Nebo, why was he seeing the promised land from Pisgah?

Some translators of the biblical book of Deuteronomy translate Pisgah (Hebrew: הַפִּסְגָּה) as a name of a mountain, usually referring to Mount Nebo. The word הַפִּסְגָּה means "summit." The region lies directly east of the Jordan River and just northeast of the Dead Sea. So, Moses climbed Nebo to its Pisgah or summit and looked across the Jordan into the promised land.

Did Moses lead the Israelites across the Red Sea, the Red Sea, or the Lake of Tanis?

Carl Drews is an ocean modeler who theorizes, in his book <u>Between Migdol and the Sea, *crossing the Red Sea with faith and Science*</u>, that the body of water that Moses led the Israelites across was not the Red Sea that is near Suez but a brackish lake, called the Lake of Tanis or the Reed Sea.

Tanis is more of a lagoon than a lake. It is formed by the Nile passing through a basin. The flow slows as it passes through, allowing sediment to settle. The sediment is rich red loamy soil constantly covered by a few feet of water; the reddish tent of the earth caused the locals to refer to the lagoon as the red sea. The loam is also a perfect environment for reeds. The reeds cover the lagoon giving it a secondary name of the sea of reeds.

Drews theory that the Israelites crossed the Suez finger of the Red Sea just east of Cairo, Egypt, is not defensible for the following reasons.

1). To believe Drews, one must disregard the biblical account of this miracle. Exodus 12:51: And on <u>that same day</u>, the Lord brought the sons of Israel out of the land of Egypt by their hosts.

God said he brought the Israelites out of Egypt on the very same day they left.

Thus, according to Scripture, the Red Sea crossing happened <u>after they had left Egypt</u>. The border of Egypt at that time was the Suez finger of the Red Sea. Any place the Israelites would have crossed the sea in this area, they would still have been in Egypt and not outside of it.

2). The lakes and lagoons around Egypt where Drews says they crossed are much too shallow to have drowned the pursuing Egyptians. If part of the theory is not valid, then is not all the theory questionable?

In the interest of transparency, there has been no archaeological evidence supporting this or any other Red Sea crossing location.

On 24 October 2014, the website *World News Daily Report* (WNDR) published an article reporting that chariot wheels and the bones of horses and men had been discovered at the bottom of the Red Sea, thereby supposedly providing archaeological proof of the Biblical narrative about the escape of the Israelites from the Egyptians.

However, according to Snopes, "if one is looking for news of an important scientific or historical discovery, *World News Daily Report* is not the place to look. WNDR is a fake news site whose own disclaimer notes that the site's articles are satirical:

World News Daily Report is a news and political satire web publication, which may or may not use real names, often in semi-real or mostly fictitious ways. All news articles contained within worldnewsdailyreport.com are fiction and presumably fake news. Any resemblance to the truth is purely coincidental, except for all references to politicians and celebrities, in which case they are based on real people but still based almost entirely in fiction.

Despite WNDR's framing of the alleged "discovery" as recent and newly announced, reports of divers finding chariot wheels and the like under the Red Sea are a hoax."

Okay, but to that, I would offer this in response; just because the remains of the Egyptian Army has not yet been found does not mean they aren't lying there at the bottom of these two thousand five hundred deep trenches waiting for He who put them there to allow their discovery.

4) Exodus 13:18-22: Hence, God led the people around by the way of the wilderness to the Red Sea.

These verses clearly reveal that the Israelites walked a long way traveling both day and night through a wilderness before crossing the Red Sea. Because the Red Sea crossing miracle happened several days after the Exodus, it couldn't have happened at the Suez finger of the Red Sea because Goshen is just 20 miles (32 km.) from the sea, just a few hours walk.

Moreover, between Goshen and the believed traditional crossing place of the Red Sea is not a wilderness.

The Suez finger of the Red Sea is about 72 miles (116 km.) south of Goshen (the place where the Israelites lived and departed Egypt). However, the land directly east of Goshen is dry and easily crossable.

The Israelites had exited Egypt on the same day they left. The route directly east of Goshen would have allowed them to leave Egypt on dry ground. Afterward, they would have been in the wilderness of Sinai, which fits well with the biblical narrative, as we will see in the next point.

5) In 1 Kings 9:26, Yam Suph refers again to the northern tip of the Aqaba Finger of the Red Sea and is where Solomon had a fleet of ships stationed at Eloth, which is modern-day Eilat.

Therefore, the term Yam Suph means reeds and also refers to the area east of Egypt. The term is mainly used to refer to the Aqaba finger of the Red Sea.

Taking this into account, the Aqaba Finger of the Red Sea is referred to as Yam Suph in the Bible.

Nuweiba Beach is in this area. The beach at Nuweiba is large, flat, and sandy, the perfect place for the 2.5 to 3 million Israelites to camp.

The ocean floor of the Red Sea by Nuweiba Beach gradually goes down and then climbs up to the shore of Saudi Arabia. Just north or south of this area, there are deep impassible ravines on the ocean floor. The Nuweiba Beach location is the only place on the Aqaba finger of the Red Sea that would have allowed the Israelites to cross. It seems reasonable to suggest that God, in His sovereignty, divinely created this sandy, graded crossing place for the Israelites to use for this magnanimous miracle.

Exodus 15:10: *You blew with Your wind, the sea covered them; They sank like lead in the mighty waters.*

Isaiah 51:10: *Was it not You who dried up the sea, the waters of the great deep; who made the depths of the sea a pathway For the redeemed to cross over?*

Steep rocky slopes form the approach to Nuweiba Beach. The Hebrews were funneled onto the beach, passing through the opening between these slopes, hemming them in. Once on the beach, there were but two ways off it, back the way they came or through the waters.

The terrain continued into the water forming a funnel or trench some 2,500 feet deep; across this finger of the sea. Steep walls on either side and level ground create the floor of the trench.

Exodus 14:29: *But the sons of Israel walked on dry land through the midst of the sea, and the waters were like a wall to them on their right hand and on their left.*

6) The Hebrews were on the beach and, thinking they were trapped, cried out to Moses as they saw the Egyptian army approaching. But God had set the trap knowing what the hard-hearted Pharaoh would think... Exodus 14:1–3: *Then the Lord said to Moses, "Tell the people of Israel to turn back and encamp in front of Pi-hahiroth, between Migdol and the sea, in front of Baal-zephon; you shall encamp facing it, by the sea. For Pharaoh will say of the people of Israel, 'They are wandering in the land; the wilderness has shut them in.*

Exodus 14:13-14: But Moses said to the people, "*Do not fear! Stand by and see the salvation of the Lord, which He will accomplish for you today; for the Egyptians whom you have seen today, you will never see them again forever. The Lord will fight for you and you shall hold your peace.*

God had a plan and executed it perfectly, as He divided the waters, dried up the seafloor with an East wind so that the Hebrews could cross over on dry land, hemmed in by the walls of water pushed up against the mountains forming their passageway.

The Egyptians followed them in, but alas, the Hebrews were up the slope quickly on foot while the heavily ladened chariots were slowed in the climb, and the waters came crashing down from the mountaintops covering the Egyptians.

So, historians, scholars, and biblical writers have had their say in the life and times of Moses. We have reviewed much of each.

My decision is to write this novel from the perspective of Moses as depicted in scripture. *Each reader will reach their own decision on how much weight to give to each question. This* novel will make the journey enjoyable.

The time is 1393 B.C. We are in the north of Egypt, in the delta area ruled by Seti, son of Ramses I and father of Ramses II. Come, go with me as we explore

MOSES: PRINCE OF EGYPT~ SON OF ABRAHAM

Dedication

This novel is dedicated to the memory of my mother,
Florence Clark Bangs, March 10, 1926-June 8, 2011.

Opening Scriptures

So, ...Joseph dwelt in Egypt, he, and his father's household. And Joseph lived one hundred and ten years. And Joseph said to his brethren, '*I am dying; but God will surely visit you and bring you out of this land to the land of which He swore to Abraham, to Isaac, and to Jacob.*' Genesis 50:22-24 (selected verses, NJK)

And Joseph died, all his brothers and all their generation. But the children of Israel were faithful and increased abundantly...Now there rose a new king over Egypt who did not know Joseph, and he said to his people, '*Look, the people of the children of Israel are more and mightier than we...then the King of Egypt spoke to the Hebrew midwives...when you do the duties of a midwife for the Hebrew women and see them on the birthstools if it is a son, then you shall kill him; but if it is a daughter, then she shall live...So Pharoah commanded all his people, saying, "Every son who is born you shall cast into the river and every daughter you shall save alive."* (Exodus 1:6-22 selected verses NKJ)

Chapter One

A Son Is Born

The morning sun pushed past the blanket hanging over the opening cut into the mud hut wall. The dust-laden rays crossed the room, probing the darkness to find the pallet where Jochabed, the pregnant wife of Amram, lay. She rolled onto her side, presenting her back to the interlopers.

A sharp pain wrapped around her abdomen and raced up her spine to spread across her chest. Jochebed screamed, and twisted again to lay on her back.

As she did, her water broke and flooded the blanket beneath her. She felt the second contraction start and arched her back, lifting her hips off the soggy sheet.

The pain rolled down her legs. She collapsed onto the pallet and rolled onto her right side as hot vomit spewed from her belly, through her mouth and nose onto the dirt floor.

Miriam turned from the cooking stone where she was heating bread for the morning meal, "Mother?"

"Jochebed said, "It is time; the baby is coming. Hand me some cold water to rinse my mouth and go get your father."

Miriam handed her mother a gourd filled with cold water and watched as she rinsed the bitterness from her mouth. A gust of cold wind swept through the open doorway, and Miriam moved to pull the covering over the door.
"No, leave it, let the cold air in; it soothes my nausea," Jochebed said.

Miriam rested a hand on her mother's head and asked, "Will you be okay if I leave you?"

"Yes, this is the beginning. It will take a while. Now go get him, but don't let anyone hear you say the baby is coming."

Seti has issued a decree that all male babies will be killed. The guards are checking each house daily; they are watching closely. I don't want the guards bashing my child against the stones.

Miriam rushed from the hut and turned to the river, where she knew her father would be gathering water to mix with the straw and mud to meet the day's quota of bricks. She saw AMRAM and her brother AARON scooping water into the stone urns as she approached the river.

The chatter of the men working alongside her father ceased as they saw her approach. Amram turned and stepped away from the water to his daughter.

"Why are you here?" Amram asked.

"Mother is in labor. She needs you."

Amram shushed her and whispered, "I cannot go, the guards would demand an explanation, and no matter what I said, they would follow me to the house to see what was happening. That would mean sure death if the child is a boy.
You will have to manage this with your mother. Take care that no one knows."

"But I don't know what to do, father."

"It will come to you; instinct will take over. Just remember, you receive the baby, and your mother delivers it.

As soon as you have him or her in your hands, be sure the airways are clear, and the baby is breathing. Your mother will tell you how to cut the cord. Make her as comfortable as you can, and I will be home for lunch. Now go."

Miriam was moving away from the river when a guard stopped her and demanded why she was there.

"My mother's cycle has come, and she is bleeding heavily. I wanted my father to come home, but he said he could not come until lunch. Will you come and help me with her?"

"What? You want me to come to a woman in her time of impurity? Get away from me."

Miriam smiled as she trotted back to the family hut.
His mother frowned when Miriam told her what her father had said.

"Very well, heat some water, get some clean cloth and two pieces of that ribbon your father bought me for my birthday.

Move those two stools together so I can sit with one hip on each. The baby will drop between them; you will have to catch him as he drops."

Miriam moved the birthing stools into place and helped her mother squat on them.

Her mother said to her, "Miriam, scoop the soil away, create a hole so that the placenta will fall into it. The baby will come, and then the placenta will follow; we will have to dispose of it, so the guards do not know a child has been born. "

"How long until the baby comes?"

"I don't know for sure; you came quickly. Your brother took five hours. But my contractions are already lasting less than a minute and are about three minutes apart, which means the labor is well advanced. This baby will be here before your father is home for lunch."

Miriam moved to the door and dropped the curtain into place so no one could see inside. She then sat down and waited.

Her mother's hot breath bathed her face as another pain hit her. Then she heard, "Here he comes, Miriam, catch him in the clean cloth."

And there he was, a bloody mass of wrinkled flesh. Miriam cupped his head in her hands and gently drew him from his mother. She made sure he was breathing and wrapped him in the clean cloth.

"What now, mom?"

“Now the placenta will follow; take it in your hands and pull gently to ensure that all of it comes out of me.”

"It can feel it now." Miriam gagged as she guided the placenta from her mother into the hole, she had scooped in the dirt floor.

"Good Miriam, now dip the cloth in the warm water. Bath your brother and remove all the blood and afterbirth from him. Clean his eyes thoroughly; make sure his airways are unobstructed."

"Grasp the umbilical cord gently. You will feel the pulse and vibration. The vibration will stop in about five minutes. Then we will tie the strings on the umbilical cord three inches apart. Take the knife, pass the blade through the flame to disinfect it, and cut the cord halfway between each string. The cord will bleed a little, don't worry about that. There are no nerves in the umbilical cord, so the baby will not feel it."

Miriam followed her mother's instructions and was holding her baby brother when her father and older brother came into the darkroom for their lunch break.

"Behold your son, husband," Jochabed said.

Amram took his son, lifted above his head, and said,
"This child will not be able to receive the blessing of the eighth day because of Pharaoh's decree, but for now, I will pray:

"God of Abraham, God of Isaac, and God of Jacob, righteous and holy Father of our Lord Yeshua, the Messiah, we acknowledge that children are a gift from you; the fruit of the womb is a reward that You give.

Like arrows in the hand of a warrior, so are the children of one's youth. How blessed is the man and woman whose quiver is full of them! May we rejoice in this child, as written: Let your parents be happy; let your mother thrill for joy.

Adon Olam, Ruler of Heaven and Earth, sustain this child for his father and mother. May (this son) fulfill his destiny.

In Your great mercy, O Lord, our God, give him a pure and holy heart to serve you throughout his life. May he become great in Your Torah.

May his heart be opened to understanding your Word, to learn and teach, and to keep and practice it. May he enter a life of good deeds and a good marriage if it is Your will.

May he enter into the New Covenant and the salvation found in Messiah, Yeshua. May he grow up to be a faithful son who forever remains within Your house.

May he be blessed in this life and be rewarded with eternal life in the world to come!

Our son, we, your parents, present you this day to the Lord. Like Samuel before you, may you always be dedicated to Him.

The kingdom of God belongs you those like you! May He who blessed the fathers, Abraham, Isaac, and Jacob, and brought a Savior to their children, may He bless this child who was dedicated to the living and eternal God this day.

May the Lord bless you and keep you. The Lord make His face shine on this child and be gracious to you.

May the Lord lift His countenance on you and give you peace.

Our father and our King, May Your grace and favor and blessing rest upon this family all the days of their lives! Amen."

"Miriam, you make sure your mother is cared for this afternoon, keep the curtain drawn, and if anyone comes, show them the bloody cloth there and tell them she is impure. They will not want to enter. Keep the baby out of sight.

"What will we call him, my wife?"

"He is our son, born here in Egypt; we will call him Mosheh, for I believe he will be a deliverer of our people."

"Father, the guards have seen mother and know that she was pregnant. When they see her next, they will she has delivered the child. Won't they demand to see the baby?"

"Maybe. We will dress her in robes and do our best to conceal that she has delivered the baby. We will need to find a place to hide him so the guards will not see him when they glance in to conduct the daily headcount."

"Hide him? Where we be able to hide him here in this small space?" Jochabed asked.

"I have asked permission to bring extra bricks into our space so we can build an oven to cook on during the coming winter. We will carve out a space beneath the hearth, where we can hide him. We have three months before the first cold weather; there will be no need to build a fire in the oven until then, which gives us time to figure out what to do.

Chapter Two

The Oven

As the sun settled into the western sky, Amram filled a basket with mud and straw.

Nour, the overseer assigned to Amram's group, saw him, and asked, "What are you doing, slave?"

Amram continued to pack the basket and replied, "I am taking material to my hut so I can build an oven for cooking inside this winter."

"Who gave you permission to take the materials for your personal use?" Nour asked.

"Rashida, the chief officer of this watch, gave me permission."

"And did he give your son, Aaron, permission also?"

"Yes, master, he did. He said we could each fill one basket at the end of each day."

"Well, hurry and fill your baskets. The crocodiles come out of the water when the sun goes down. I want to get away from this river before dark."

Amram and Aaron filled their baskets and hurried to their hut.

Amram sat beside the stone hearth at the door of their hut and fashioned the mud and straw into six bricks. He sat them on the hearth and added sticks to the fire to make it even hotter.

Aaron followed his father's example and asked, "dad, how long will it take for us to have enough bricks to build the oven inside the hut?"

"Two months will give us seven hundred and twenty bricks. We can build a small oven with seven hundred; we will use the extra twenty for a hearth in front of the oven."

Amram finished fashioning his bricks and laid them on the back of the cooking stone. "Son, lay yours beside these but leave enough room for Miriam to heat our evening meal. Each night the heat from the stone will set them. We will leave them here while we work, and the heat of the summer days will continue to harden them. Soon we will have enough to fashion the base of the oven; we will hide Moses behind the base."

"Here comes the night watch to conduct the headcount. Continue what you are doing. Say nothing; I will answer them if they question what we are about."

Aaron continued to fashion the brick as the detail approached, "Here Hebrew, what are you doing?" the Egyptian asked.

"We are fashioning brick to use in building an oven for our hut, master. Rashida has permitted us to do so," Amram answered, waving his hand to indicate the line of huts to his right and left.

"Why do you need an oven inside the hut?"

"We don't in the summer. But in the winter, especially during the rainy months, it helps us to be able to cook our meals inside, plus it provides warmth for the hut."

"Okay, my list says there should be four Hebrews for this hut; I see you two, where are the other two?"

"My wife and daughter are inside, master. My wife is in her time of impurity. Do you want me to call her out for you to see her?"

"No. Enter a count of four for this hut," he said to the Egyptian keeping the record, and moved to the next hut

Chapter Three

Hiding Moses

"Hand me another brick, son."

Aaron handed his father the brick and said, "This one is still warm, Father. I hope we are not rushing this too much."

"It does not matter; this is the last one, and we will put it here on top, well supported by the solid base."

"Miriam, you are small enough, work your way behind the oven, lay Moses in the space we have carved out, and let's see how this works."

"Yes, Father, let me check the cavity first. I have killed several spiders and a scorpion in the last two days, and I can't stand the thought of him being bitten by one."

"Hurry, child; I want him hidden before the night watch comes for the headcount."

Miriam slipped behind the oven, and Aaron handed her the blankets for Moses. She smoothed them out on the floor and reached for Moses. She lay him on his blankets and moved out from behind the oven.

The doorway curtain was thrust aside, and the night watch officer stepped into the hut, "What are you slaves doing?"

"I just now placed the last brick in our oven," Amram answered.

"Let's have a look at your work," the officer said as he stepped close to the oven and bent over it.

As he did, the scream of a child crying echoed through the hut. "What is that?" the guard asked.

"Our neighbors have a new baby daughter," Amram answered.

The guard looked at his list and said, "That's right; I see that on the list; they reported the birth last night."

He left the hut telling his assistant, "Mark, all four of these Hebrews present."

Amram sighed in relief and moved to the door to be sure the night watch had moved on.

"Okay, so we know this works. But we cannot get away with it for long. Moses is six weeks old and growing like a reed. Jochabed, I know you don't want to think about this, but we are going to have to have a plan soon."

"I have a plan, husband. I overheard Princess Hatshepsut when she and her handmaidens were bathing in the river. She wants a child, but she is married to her half-brother and Seti will not allow them to have a child. I heard her praying to their God of the Nile, Hapi. Hapi is the god of fertility and Hatsheput believes he will give her a child supernaturally. I will put Moses in a basket and set him to drift into her presence the next time I see her bathing in the Nile. She will believe Hapi has sent him in answer to her prayers; draw him out and take him as her son."

"That is a risky plan, wife. The Nile is full of predators. If the basket tips over, they will eat Moses."

"No, I have thought of that. There is an inlet near where her party goes into the river. The growth of reeds hides it. I will push the basket into the current, and it will take less than one minute to float into their midst. And her guards will be in the water in front of the inlet, pounding the river with their long poles to drive the snakes and alligators away. Moses will be drawn from the water and live to rescue our people from slavery."

"How do you know that wife?"

"God gave it to me in a dream. Moses was born into captivity; he will be raised and educated in privilege and then return to lead his people into God's plan."

"The princess and Seti will know that Moses is a Hebrew child as soon as they see him. Are you sure this will work? Do you not fear that Seti will have him killed?"

"No, God has shown me that Moses will cross over the waters safely and be drawn out by the princess who will be able to persuade her father to spare his life."

"Okay, wife. Prepare your basket for him. You must cast him into the Nile within the next week. The night watch is growing suspicious."

Chapter Four

Passing through, Drawn from

Jochebed crouched in the reeds on the bank of the Nile. She could hear the splashing and laughter of Hatshepsut and her attendants who were bathing some ninety feet away. She opened the reed basket and gazed at her son one last time; she sat the basket in the Nile. She was pleased to see that it floated, and that the pitch she had coated it with was keeping the water out. She closed the basket, picked a long reed from the growth around her, and use it to push the basket into the current. The swift water swept it away downstream to where the queen and her party were. Jochabed smiled when she heard the Hatsheput say, "Look a basket. Bring it to me."

Jochabed watched the princess open the basket and say, "It is a Hebrew child. Some mother has cast him into the Nile to keep him from being killed. And Hapti has brought him to me in answer to my prayers. Hand him to me."

Jochabed heard Moses' cry and knew he was hungry. She crawled out of the reeds and slipped up the bank to where Miriam and the other Hebrew women were gathered. She watched as Queen Hatshepsut pointed to where they were standing and saw one of the attendants approaching. Miriam stepped out to meet the attendant and said, “We saw you draw the child from the river. Are you looking for a wet nurse?

"Yes, and I see that women appears to be lactating.”

“Yes Highness, her child was a son, and he was cast into the river. Her breasts are full and painful. She would be happy to nurse the child.”

"Don't call me highness. I am an attendant. Come with me."

Jochabed followed the woman to where the princess stood holding Moses.

"This is a Hebrew child; he is not yet weaned. You are lactating; I want you to be his wet nurse. You will come with me to the palace, and we will set a feeding schedule for you to come daily to nurse him; he will be my son, raised as a prince of Egypt, but for now, he will feed on the milk of his people."

She handed Moses to Jochabed and said, "Nurse him."

Jochabed bared her breast to feed Moses.

He stopped crying and began suckling.

"Look how he takes to her; it is if she is his mother. Is this your son? Did you set him afloat hoping that we would draw him from the Nile?" the princess asked.

Jochabed said, "No, highness, he is your son. I am of his people, but he will be a prince of Egypt, as you say. I will feed him as an infant, but you shall raise him as your son."

Jochabed nodded and said, "Yes, he is, and I will call him Moses because he passed over the Nile to come to me, and I drew him from it."

The queen and her party turned to walk away, and Jochabed followed with Moses. She leaned in to kiss his cheek and said, "It has been written; it shall be done. You are now in a position to lead your people from captivity.

Chapter Five

Prince of Egypt

Seti smiled as his daughter appeared at the door of his throne room. She waited with Moses, her adoptive son, in her arms.

He extended his scepter toward her, and she entered the court. Hatshepsut bowed before her father. He took Moses from her arms and sat him on Seti's lap. "He has grown daughter; I remember when you brought him to the palace. I could hold him in one hand; Now he must weigh ten to fifteen pounds or maybe more."

"Yes, Father. He was three months old when I found him in the Nile. He is now six months old. His nurse has plenty of milk for him, and he takes it all."

"Three months old when you found him. That means his parents hid him from us to avoid the royal command. He is a Hebrew and looks more and more like his nurse. I suspect she is his birth mother."

"She may have given birth to him, but I am his mother, and you are his grandfather, and I know you share my love for him."

"You know, daughter, my counselors have warned me that he may well be the one in my dream, the one the stars speak of, the one who will lead the Hebrews in rebellion to take my crown."

"Nonsense, father. He is a baby. I am raising him as a Prince of Egypt. He will serve the crown; he will defend you against any who dares to rebel against you."

Seti strolled across the room to the table where his chief astrologer sat. "What do you say you to that, astrologer? Will he steal the crown, or will he defend it?

"I confess that I do not know. I suggest a simple test Majesty. You sit on your throne and place the baby on your lap. Put a burning candle on the table before you. Set the crown beside it.

If he reaches for the fire, he is a defender; if he goes for the crown, he is the rebel leader prophesied of by the stars."

"Very well, light the candle."

When the candle was in full blaze, Seti sat on his throne and placed the crown next to the candle. The baby turned to the shining jewels and reached for them. He grabbed the crown and pulled it from the table. Moses wiggled around on Seti's lap and placed pushed the crown toward his grandfather.

"See, Father, Moses does not place the crown on his head; instead, he takes it from the flame and hands it to you. He is a defender of the crown," Hatshepsut shouted.

Seti nodded and said, "I agree, daughter. He may well have Hebrew blood, but he is a Prince of Egypt.

Seti turned to the astrologer and said, "You are a witness. I have spoken. From this moment and for as long as he lives, Moses is a Prince of Egypt.

He turned to his daughter and said, "Bring the scribes in. I want it written; Moses is a Prince of Egypt. As such, he is officially in the line of succession for the throne. Anyone who speaks against him speaks against me and the crown."

"Thank you, Majesty. But may I suggest that I am not the proper witness for such matters of state? Should you not convene your court? There will be questions concerning the line of succession, and we should have your will on record with the court present to show their advice and consent," Remy said.

The astrologer bowed and called to the guards, "Pharaoh orders his court to assemble and for his wife and son Ramses to attend his presence also. Make it happen now."

"You called me husband?" Tausert asked from the doorway.

Yes, Tuya, you may enter my presence. Come in and sit here beside me," Seti replied.

"Yes, husband, but please, you know how I hate you to call me Tuya; my name is Tausert. Can you not use my full name, especially in the presence of the court?" she asked.

"Sit down, woman, and be thankful that I allow you in my court. I will call you what I wish; I am Pharaoh."

"Majesty, your court is here," the captain of the guard called from the door.

"Yes, Sercy, be sure none have weapons and allow them to enter as you clear them, one by one," Seti responded.

"Search them, dear? Why, has there been a threat, or do you have news of a plot against you?" Tausert asked.

"No, but I am Pharaoh, and one cannot be too careful."

Seti waved the members of his court to be seated at the table and asked, "Where is Ramses, Captain? Did he not get my summons?"

"He was in his brother's chambers, Majesty. He wanted to hear what the physicians think about how Prince Amenefernebes' recovery is progressing."

"We will wait; this matter must be done properly. I want no questions as to my will in the line of succession.

"Here he comes, highness."

Seti turned to see his son at the doorway. "Enter, son."

Ramses bowed and moved to the chair Seti pointed to.

"How is your brother this morning?"

"Not well, father, the physicians have bled him and put a new load of leeches on him, but his blood remains feverish; he cannot keep food or water on his stomach. He is dehydrated and grows weaker with each hour.

The physicians believe the illness comes from drinking wine from unfired clay. They say the metals in the clay leach out into the wine, are consumed, and poison the body. They fear he will not survive."

"All the more reason that the record is clear on the line of succession."

"Scribes, it is my order that you transcribe every word I say from this point on. They are to be a part of the royal record and shall have the force of law.

Let the record show that I have called the court to order, scribes you draft in the appropriate date and time, and show that present are my advisors, my counselors, my wife, list her full name, Tausert, my daughter Hatsheput, my son Ramses II and my infant grandson, the adoptive son of my daughter as mentioned earlier. Absent is my son Amenefernebes.

I have called the court to order for the purpose of setting in place the line of succession to my throne. That line will be as follows:

My first wife, Twosert, died. Upon the death of Twosert, I named our daughter Hatsheput to replace her in all ceremonial settings; Then I decided to marry again, but Hatsheput is my regent and is first in line to succeed me as

Pharaoh, should I die before my son Amenefernebes reaches his majority. Next in line after Hatsheput is Amenefernebes, the firstborn son of Tausert and me. Following Amenefernebes is Ramses II, our second-born son.

I have these final orders for this session of the court. First, I hereby decree and declare that my daughter Hatsheput is now Queen of Egypt and will remain so until the next Pharoah succeeds me. Her adoptive son Moses, my adoptive grandson, is from this moment and for as long as he lives is a Prince of Egypt. He shall have all the opportunities and advantages of royalty; his education shall include the Military training that all children of the court have. However, since Moses is born a Hebrew, he is not and never will be in the line of succession; unless and until following Egyptian law, the full council shall, at the Pharoah's death, find the next in line to be unfit to lead and in unanimous agreement elect Moses to be Pharoah. Secondly, since my daughter is now officially first in the line of succession, I am commissioning her as an officer in the army, and my order is that she will serve as the commander of the royal military academy."

I will pause here and ask you for your comment and or consent.

"Yes, Majesty, Let the record reflect that we consent and have no advice to the contrary. But we will point out for the record that while women have held ceremonial positions in the army, no woman has ever held a command position. By appointing Hatsheput to a command position Pharaoh is breaking tradition and setting a precedent."

"Very well, your comment is noted and now the next order is to be carefully considered. Moses is a Prince of Egypt and a royal family member. Any who speaks against him speaks against the Pharaoh and the crown. Let them do so at their own peril."

Seti turned to the court and asked, "What say ye, speak now under license from your Pharaoh and hereafter hold your tongue."

Ramen stood, bowed, and said, "I will speak for the court as the chief member majesty. You are Pharaoh, and if this is your will, it shall be written, and once written, it is irreversible, as you know. Our counsel is that you consider carefully because your action here today could place a Hebrew in charge of Egypt. Is this wise? Would Egypt prosper under a Hebrew, one who was born into slavery?"

Seti had anticipated this and replied, "All one has to do is look, no matter the assignment, they excel, and we prosper from their excellence."

"True Pharaoh, but let us remember that an Egyptian is on the throne as Pharaoh."

"Well, said Ramen. With Moses, we will have one born a Hebrew, so the slaves will respect his rule and raised as a Prince of Egypt so we can trust our matters of National interest to him."

Ramen nodded and looked at his fellow advisers. They all nodded their heads in agreement with the Pharaoh.

Ramen turned back to Seti and said, "Let the record show that the court has had the opportunity to voice its' concerns, heard Pharaoh's wise response, and have no objections to his order. Let it be written as Pharaoh has said.

"Majesty, if you please highness?" Sercy called from the doorway.

"What is it, Captain?"

"Majesty, the physicians, have sent news, Amenefernebes has died. Long live his memory."

Seti turned to his wife and said, "You may go and attend to the body of our son."

Then he said, "For the record, Prince Amenefernebes has died. Ramses II takes his place in the line of succession. Ramses will also now serve as prime minister. Let it be written, let it be done."

Chapter Six

Ramsey's Prophecy to Moses

Hatsheput shrugged out of her robe and used it to wipe the steamy fog from the polished bronze standing next to the tub. she looked at her thighs, then her stomach and breasts. She turned to see her hips and murmured; I will have the maids remove this mirror. Its' report is more than I wish to receive each day.

She looked at the tub and frowned at the steam coming off the water. "Too hot again. I have told Mira that I want the bath warm, not scalding. She lowered her foot, dipped her toe, and decided to take the plunge. Stepping in, she winced, then settled into the water and slouched down until it lapped at her chin. She could feel her pores opening and lay back to soak.

A rose petal floated against her chin, and she could smell its' essence as it rode the steam into her nostrils. She smiled; this is why Mira kept her bath so hot; she wanted the heat to open the rose petals and release their nectar.

The door opened, and Mira came in. "Not yet Mira. Give me ten more minutes," Hatsheput said.

"Yes, majesty, but remember you have a meeting with the prime minister in ten minutes."

"My brother can wait. Father has named him prime minister, but he named me Queen," Hatsheput smiled.

Mira turned to leave, and as she opened the door, Hatsheput heard voices raised in argument. "Wait, Mira, who is that shouting, and what is the argument about?"

"It is Ramses and Moses, majesty. And they are arguing about the treatment of the Hebrews, again."

'Leave the door open so that I can hear them."

Hatsheput sat up in the tub and leaned forward to hear better. She recognized Moses' voice, "Okay, so they are our slaves. And as such, they have great value to the realm. They have built and maintained our infrastructure, managed our foreign trade, and balanced our books. They are assets. We should take care to guard the assets of the realm. Yet you insist on working them until they drop dead."

"Nonsense Moses. We are not hurting the Hebrews. They work all day in the hot sun and then go home and reproduce like rats. They outnumber us now. If they ever decide to join our enemies and fight against us, they will be a formidable foe."

"That has been tried before and I stand here in witness to the futility of such an effort, my brother. Why don't we take a different approach and do all we can to keep them loyal to the throne; why continue to drive this wedge between them and us?"

"We are not brothers. I am the crown Prince, soon to be Pharaoh, and you are a Hebrew, born in captivity and by sheer luck drawn from the Nile by my sister who dared not conceive a child with her husband, our half-brother Thutmose. Father ordered the marriage to keep the bloodline to the throne clear, but she fears the possible results of the inbreeding. She prayed to Hapi and went to the Nile, hoping he would answer her prayer as the god of the Nile. As luck would have it, you came floating by, and she believed you were an answer to her prayers. But your Blood is Hebrew, not Egyptian. We are not related."

Hatsheput stood in the tub, beckoned Mira to bring her a towel, and stepped from the tub into the towel as Mira wrapped it around her. Pat me dry quickly and hand me my robe."

Mira wiped the Queen down, removed the towel, and handed her the purple robe. Hatsheput walked through the door and down the hallway to where Moses and Ramses stood nose to nose.

"Enough of this. Both of you are well past forty years of age, yet you continue to argue like you did when you were ten. Ramses, Moses is your brother and a member of the royal family, so said our father, the Pharaoh, and so say the official records of his court. You are indeed the crown prince, next in the line of succession, and will be Pharaoh, but you are not yet.

Don't be so stubborn; admit that others may see things that you do not. Take counsel from those who stand with you."

"Now is as good a time as any to set this straight, Sister. Yes, Moses is a member of the royal family by our father's proclamation, but he will never be Pharaoh of Egypt. I am not yet, but as you say, I will be one day.

I will be Pharaoh because I am the son of Pharaohs; I have the Blood of Pharaohs. Moses is a Hebrew; he is the son of their father, Abraham. You have tried to graft him into our family, but the graft did not, will not take because he does not have our Blood. The proclamation may say that he is a Prince of Egypt, but his Blood says that he is a son of Abraham.

Next, although father named you Queen, I will not. As soon as I am Pharaoh, your reign ends. You are my sister by Blood, and you will remain a member of the royal family, but I will name Haman to be my prime minister and commander of the armies.

As for the Hebrews, they are slaves, Father and I agree on this. His love for Moses has blinded father, but I believe that the day is coming when Moses will no longer be able to hide the fact that he is more Hebrew than Egyptian in his heart. On that day, father's blindness will cease; and he will see Moses for what he is, a Hebrew.

Show me if I am wrong, Moses. Get out of the palace and walk among the Hebrews and those who manage them on a day-to day basis. Look, listen, and learn; these are stubborn and prideful people. If we do not apply the whip, they will sit down or, worse, sabotage us by using inferior building materials so that the infrastructure will fail. Perhaps you will come to support the kingdom rather than your fellow Hebrews. I hope so, but I believe your past is an indicator of your future; you hear but do not follow instructions. You tend to disregard instruction and act as you think best, which, I prophesy, will prove to be the very thing that will keep you from fulfilling your destiny. I predict Moses that your inattention to detail will cause you to be left behind while others step in to complete your assignment.

I hope I have made my position clear. Now, you may leave my presence."

Chapter Seven

The Queen Instructs Her Son

Moses stood with Hatsheput listening to the sound of Ramses' sandals against the marble floor as he stomped down the hallway. "Wow, he acts as if he is already pharaoh."

"That's because he is, my son. Seti sits on the throne, but Ramses stands beside him as his prime minister. Ramses knows fathers' philosophy of government and makes sure to voice his support daily. Father loves him as his son, but he also values him as a trusted adviser. Ramses is preparing the court for his reign; they accept him already.

"And his statement that he will end your reign as queen. Can he do that?"

"Yes, as soon as he is pharaoh, he can name his cabinet. those in his favor are rewarded, those who are not must bow before his will, if they are to live in his realm, under his reign."

"So, mother, which group am I in?"

"You are in that group that needs to bow and serve. I suggest you let him see you walking among the Hebrews and show him by your actions that you want to be Egyptian more than you want to be Hebrew. Make no mistake, Moses, Ramses does not trust you, and your future is literally in his hands."

"Surely you do not believe that Ramses will try to kill me, mother?"

"No, you enjoy the protection of royalty, Even Ramses does not dare breach the protective covering you enjoy from father. But beware, this suggestion he made today offering you the opportunity to prove him wrong by walking among the slaves and their masters is wrought with danger. He believes that putting you in their midst as they are disciplined by the overseers when they fail to meet their production goals will cause you act impulsively to protect the slaves. An intemperate act against the overseer who represents the pharaoh could be seen as treason. Treason would cause you to be expelled from the family and make you an enemy of the realm. You must not allow the passion of an instant cancel the promise of your future."

"Mother, I cannot be a counterfeit. I am a Hebrew, bone, and blood of the tribe of Levi. I will not abandon my people. I will not stand by and see them brutalized by anyone and that includes Ramses.

"Moses, you distress me. I fear Ramses prophesy will be fulfilled."

Chapter Eight

The Queen Mother

Hatsheput woke early. She sat up on her couch and called for Mira. "Yes majesty?" Mira said from the doorway.

"Good morning Mira, take a message to Moses for me. Tell him to join me at court this morning. Tell him I said not to go among the slaves until after we speak with pharaoh."

Hatsheput dressed, ate a quick breakfast, and moved down the hallway into the court chambers. Her footsteps echoed in the empty chamber. She walked to her chair, sitting across the chamber, directly opposite her father's throne. He had it moved from beside his throne where a wife queen would have sat.

Hatsheput heard steps approaching and turned to see her brother enter the chamber. "Good morning brother," she greeted him.

"Good morning sister," he replied. "It is early; you must have important business before the court."

"Yes, brother, I am glad you are here. I came early hoping to have the ear of pharaoh before the court assembles. It is good that you are here, you can add your thoughts to mine. We can speak with our father, the pharaoh in family council."

Ramses smiled and said, "I would guess that this family council concerns Moses in some way."

"Yes, I heard your suggestion that he walk among the slaves and observe the way we oversee them. I agree with you that Moses needs to do this, that he needs to do all that he can to show that his loyalty lies with the realm and not the Hebrews.

Ramses nodded and asked, "Does Moses not need to be here for this?"

"I have sent for him."

"And I am here. Good morning mother, good morning Ramses. I did not call you brother, because you have instructed me not to."

"Enough, please! Let's not argue."

"Indeed!"

Hatsheput stood and bowed as her father entered the chamber and sat on his throne.

"Good morning pharaoh," Ramses said.

"Why are my children gathered here so early? My guess is that you come not to speak with Pharaoh, but to your father and grandfather. Am I right?"

"You are as perspective as ever father. Ramses has suggested to Moses that there are those who question his loyalty, whether it lies with his lineage or with you as his pharaoh. He suggested that Moses walk among the slaves and their overseers daily, that he observes the work, the discipline applied to keep the slaves at their task, to offer suggestions on how to make the effort more efficient and to support the realm in those endeavors. I am concerned that this could be misinterpreted as his seeking to interfere with the work of the crown, to gain favor with the slaves and lead them in revolt against pharaoh.

I am here to ask pharaoh to endorse Ramses' suggestion so all will know that Moses is acting in concert with your will."

Seti nodded and asked, "And you Ramses? Did you make this suggestion and if so for what reason?"

"Yes, pharaoh. Sister is correct in all she has said. I think it would be good for people to see that Moses acts in support of the crown. I think it would be helpful for pharaoh to endorse the undertaking this morning before the court."

"And you Moses, what do you have to say?"

"I am your majesty's servant. I am most pleased that the crown prince trusts me to perform this service for the crown."

"Very well, I know there is more to this than I am being told, but I don't have the time nor the inclination to hear any more of this. I will do as you all wish. But one thing I do want explained, briefly. I heard Moses say to you Ramses that he did not call you brother because you instructed him not to. I want a yes or no answer. Is this true?"

"Yes father, I am not his brother, I am the crown prince next in the line of succession to your throne. I do not wish there to be any confusion on that point."

"Nonsense Ramses. To suggest the possibility of confusion says that I as pharaoh have not made the line of succession clear. I know you would not make such a rash suggestion. Am I correct?"

"Yes, and I beg pharaoh's forgiveness. I will avoid any future such conversation to prevent my statements being misconstrued."

"Excellent, now your pharaoh speaks from a fathers' heart, but as a command nonetheless, it is my wish that you and Moses heal this breach and do so quickly.

Both of you listen carefully to me. You will suppress the rivalry, the incident during your last military training exercise created a rift in the court. Surely you must know that people being people, there are members of the court who favor Moses and those who favor Ramses.

I will not have the court divided; and this open conflict, if allowed to continue, would surely bring it.

I am asking you two to sit and think about how that incident came about, examine it in detail and think about what you can do to avoid it happening again.

One last thing, my daughter. You have come here today to have your father's ear. You have succeeded. But let me say this, you are both queen and mother. But this is the last time you will be allowed to act before pharaoh as queen mother. Am I clear?"

"Yes pharaoh, thank you father."

Excellent. Moses you will start your duties for the crown first thing tomorrow morning. Daughter, the queen will not be needed at court this morning, you may leave our presence. Ramses, you will remain."

Moses bowed before his grandfather and then his mother. He backed out of the chamber so as not to turn his back to the Pharoah. He waited in the hallway as his mother took her leave of the Pharaoh.

Hatsheput turned to face Moses as she left the chamber. "Come walk with me. Don't say anything until we are well away from the doorway."

Moses followed her onto the balcony overlooking the Nile. She stepped aside and motioned for Moses to follow her into the recessed area where the couches were shaded from the morning sun. "Sit here close to me Moses, I do not want to be overheard."

"What is wrong mother? Why are you being so secretive?"

"Because I can see that you do not realize Ramses' intent. Your grandfather spoke of it, but you paid no attention. Ramses does not see you as a rival, he sees you as an enemy. You made a fool of him in the military exercise father spoke of. Some members of the court did indeed take your side and suggest openly that you would make a better commander of the army than he. Those comments stung him. He sees you as a contender for the crown and will stop at nothing to remove you from contention."

Your grandfather is trying his best to allay his fears, that is why he kept him in the court and sent you out this morning. I want you to avoid him the rest of the day. Go to your quarters, think through the military exercise, go over it in your mind detail by detail. Think about what led up to it, how it unfolded and what you could have done to prevent it from happening the way it did."

"But mother."

"No, but mother. You are in peril. Now go and do what I told you. There is a storm coming so it is a good day to be inside anyway."

****

Moses watched her walk away. *'She really believes I am in danger.'* He mused.

He stood and trudged to his quarters. The approaching storm had darkened the sky, Moses lit an oil lamp and sat on his couch. His eyes grew heavy as the rain began to beat a slow steady rhythm on the roof over his quarters. The rain had ridden in on a cool north breeze and Moses lay back on his couch and pulled a light gauze covering over his legs. He thought of what his mother had said and allowed his mind to go back to the night they returned from the exercise. Ramses had accused Moses of treason for exposing him to ridicule by bringing him to the palace bound with ropes. Moses had presented Ramses to the General as a prisoner of war and proof that he was the victor in the exercise. *'Probably should have not done that,'* was the last conscious thought Moses had before sleep claimed him. He relived that night in his dreams.

After presenting Ramses to the General, Moses had retired to his quarters for some much-needed rest. Tired as he was, Sleep still eluded Moses. His cramping legs were restless, twitching and forcing him to shift and turn, seeking a position of comfort. His suffering body refused to allow his mind to sleep.

A spear of light parted the darkness, the following crash of the thunder shook the room, and a gust of wind pushed a wave of cold rain past the drapes, driving Moses from his bed. He had moved to a chair in the far corner of the room, safe from the wind-driven rain, and sat with his head in his hands.

Once again, he brought the events of the past day's training exercise up for review. General Patie was him and his classmates as hard as he dared. These were not ordinary young cadets striving for a commission in Pharaoh's Army; these were the privileged children and

Grand children of the royal family and Pharoah's court. It was understood that from this class would come the future leaders of government and the military who would preserve and defend Seti's dynasty. Ramses II, Pharaoh's son, and heir to the throne, was among the students. Ramses II and the other students made little effort to hide their resentment that Moses, a Hebrew by birth and blood, was included. Some even expressed their concern about a non-Egyptian being groomed to hold a command position in the Egyptian Army. But, Seti had made Moses a member of the royal family and a Prince of Egypt by decree.

Pharaoh ordered General Patie to show no leniency to these royal children. He wanted them pushed to the breaking point, to make decisions under extreme duress to learn from their mistakes in training to avoid them on the battlefield.

Patie took his orders seriously. The day had started with a fifteen-mile march to a desert oasis along the border with Ethiopia. A mock village complete with citizens and livestock had been erected.

The officer candidates were divided into two groups. One group, commanded by Ramses II, played the part of Ethiopian raiders who were to wait until dark and then attack the village.

The second group led by Moses were dispatched on a routine patrol to the border five miles North and west of the village. They were to scout the frontier, observe the Ethiopians' activity, and then return before nightfall; Patie stressed that the attack would begin after dark; therefore,

Moses had to lead his group at route march pace or 180 steps a minute to meet this deadline. The trainees groaned when they heard this. The fifteen-mile march had left them weak.

Patie ordered Moses and the defenders to repel the raiders and then to pursue and punish them for the incursion. He reminded Moses and Ramses that they would be operating near the international border at night. He stressed how important it was for them to maintain operational awareness to not to cross the border. He made clear that the trainees were to honor the Ethiopian sovereignty. Then he ordered the trainees to surrender their weapons and replaced them with wooden swords, wooden spears, and blunted arrows.

Ramses led his raiders into the desert as instructed. But he did not follow the orders to go three miles into the desert. A mile out, he led his raiders into a wadi and waited until he was sure Moses, and his men were well away from the village on their routine patrol. He then attacked the town. Patie watched, wondering how Moses would handle this turn of events. The raiders rounded up the citizens and their livestock and pushed them out of the oasis toward the border.

Moses slowed his pace as he neared the border. He kneeled behind a dune and waved his men to form a circle around him. He waited a minute, listening to the men gasping for breath, '*They are done. I will keep this simple, make a short foray along the border, and then lead them back.*' he thought.

Moses leaned forward, pointed over his shoulder toward the border, and whispered, "The border is there. You will see the watchtowers as soon as we step from behind this dune. The guards will see us and send an alert to their reserves. We want them to know that we are on a routine patrol and pose no threat. When we stand, I will call you to order loud enough that they can hear us. We will march out, turn to the east and walk along the border for three miles. We will move slowly, use the time to catch our breath, and gather ourselves for the run back to the village. We must be in the village before dark. Ramses will raid the village as soon as the sunsets.

Moses waited a few minutes longer until the gasping for breath abated, then stood and, in a loud voice, commanded them to form up. He led his defenders out into the open and, as expected, the border guards began hoisting flags to the top of their towers, signaling their response team that an Egyptian unit was patrolling along the border.

Moses led his patrol along the Egyptian side of the border at a slow, measured pace. Three miles from their observation point, he turned them left and moved them toward the village at route pace.

Moses stumbled; his legs were leaden, his throat was parched from sucking in the hot desert air, his lungs cramped demanding oxygen, and he could feel his pulse pounding behind his eyes. He glanced back at his defenders and was disappointed to see that they were strung out behind him. He waited on one knee while they came to him. He waved them forward and climbed the dune. His heart sank; before him lay the ruins of the village. He moved forward, taking care to examine the tracks. He could tell that they were hours old. Ramses had ignored the orders and raided the village long before dark.

Moses felt his rage building and forced himself to relax and think, 'Ramses knew the general would not interfere with him, would not dare risk displeasing his future Pharaoh.

He will not stop at this early attack; he will do all he can to make me look bad. He will hide the villagers and livestock where it will be most difficult for me to rescue them. That means he will or has crossed the border and is hiding in the valley below the Ethiopian border command center. Patie has ordered us not to cross the border; he has taken our weapons, so I will not take my men into harm's way; I will entice Ramses to come to me. How? Using his greatest weakness, his vanity.'

Moses gathered his defenders and outlined his Plan by saying, "Ramses has shown his disdain for me and you by ignoring Patie's orders, he attacked the village well before dark knowing that we had to run to the border, patrol for three miles, and then run back to the village. He is counting on us being too tired to pursue him.

He knew the general would not challenge him because he is a future Pharoah. But he is not Pharoah yet; we can still expose his callous disregard of orders and show Seti how little he cares for those he commands. We may well effect change in Ramses behavior and in doing so save lives; for one day he will lead Egyptians in actual battle."

Moses paused and glanced at the exhausted men before him. They had collapsed on the ground, yet he could see a desire for retribution in their eyes. He waited, letting that desire feed on the humiliation Ramses had visited on them.

Merkel spoke, "Yes, let's do this. Ramses is my blood kin, and one day will be my Pharoah. When that time comes, I will serve him faithfully, as will each of you, but he needs to understand that although we will not be Pharoah, we have value and deserve his respect. What do you purpose, Moses?

Moses moved closer to the men, kneeled, and called them to form a circle around him. He smoothed the san in front of him and, using his finger, drew a map of the area he believed Ramses to be hiding in. "I believe Ramses has crossed the border and is hiding here in this depression between these two watchtowers. He knows I will not disobey Patie, and if by some chance I did, he is counting on the guards in the watchtowers to see us and react, giving him time to move the villagers. His vanity will not permit him to consider the possibility of failure. We will exploit that."

"We will use the cover of darkness to work our way near the first border watchtower. I will lead half of our group forward and pause behind the same dune we used for concealment earlier today. We will form up then break from cover, charging toward the border as if we intend to capture the guard tower in a pre-emptive invasion strike. But we will slow our pace enough to allow the guards in the tower to light their signal fires; Ramses will see the warning and break from his hiding spot to cross the border before he can be caught by the forces who will respond to the alarm. Remember, he is hiding in this depression; it is more of a trough than depression, and it rises like a ramp up out of the depression at the point where it crosses the border. He can stay below grade and out of sight until he crosses out of Ethiopia and comes up on level ground in Egypt. That is a plus, but it is also his only option because he will be closed in by rather steep banks with sandstone outcroppings. He will not try to climb out with the livestock and the villagers, especially in the dark. He will follow the trough to her where it rises out of the depression, cross the border, and run for the village to claim victory before the general. That is where Merkel will be waiting with the other half of our force. Use the darkness as cover and deploy your force so that you can spring the trap on him as he is climbing up out of the trough. Be prepared to use force because Ramses will not want to be taken. You must put him on the ground; and bind him. Those with him will surrender as soon as you take Ramses. Do not linger; move the villagers and the livestock away from the border and run for the village. The Ethiopians will send a rapid response force when they see the guard tower alert. You must get away from the border before they reach your position. We will swing in behind you to serve as a rearguard in the event the Ethiopians choose to pursue you.

We will link up at the village and present our prize, bound and humbled to the general." Moses paused and looked at his defenders. They were smiling and nodding in agreement.

Moses stood and said, "Choose your team Mekel, the rest will go with me."

The two men clasped hands and moved into the darkness.

Moses and his team gathered behind the sand dune. The night was not a dark as Moses had hoped, the moon seemed to be shinning directly down on Moses and his team. He glanced to the west and saw a bank of low clouds scudding across the sky, *'the winds aloft are pushing those clouds at a fairly fast pace, they will be over us in three to five minutes, they will blot out the moon light providing a brief shadow between here and the border. We will use that shadow as cover to advance toward the border, when the cloud passes, we will be in plain sight and the guards will signal the alarm,'* Moses mused.

He beckoned his team close and whispered his plan. Every head tilted to the sky watching the approaching clouds, as soon as they slid between the moon and the team, Moses led them from behind the sand dune and jogged toward the border. The clouds were gone as quickly as they had come. The moon's light beamed down and bounced off the armor Moses and his team wore. The guards in the tower saw them immediately. Moses smiled as he heard the guards excited shouts. He broke into a full run toward the border. He saw the first signal lantern blaze to life and watched as it was hoisted to the top of the tower. Three other lanterns followed up the ropes quickly. As soon as the signal lamps were hoisted, Moses turned and led his team parallel to the border. They ran easily over the flat sandy terrain and were soon at the ramp leading up out of the trough. Moses laughed at the sight of Ramses, struggling against the bindings that held him captive on the ground.

"What have we here?" he asked Mekel pointing at Ramses. What we have here my friend is our classmate the future Pharoah of Egypt. Seems he lost his way on this dark night and ended up in yon trough in the Ethiopian earth. We have rescued him, but I fear in the dark he mistook us for an enemy. We found it necessary to bind him to prevent injury. But now that he can see we are friends and not foes, should we release him, Moses?"

"Release me at once or I swear you will regret it, Moses. You know that binding me, the crown prince is treasonus." Ramses fumed.

"No Ramses, I will not release you. I will take you to the palace and present you to Pharaoh as proof of our victory. I do so because I know that given a chance you would concoct some tale to deny these men their due. But I promise you that I will not expose your treachery and disobedience of the generals' orders. That will be between you, the general and Pharaoh. Nevertheless, let you and I have this understanding from hence forth, there is to be no trust between the two of us."

Moses ordered the defenders to place Ramses in a cart and set out for the palace.

As the troop neared the palace Moses felt a check in his spirit, *'Should I free Ramses, or should I continue with him bound?'* he asked himself. He looked at the faces of the defenders, saw how erect they held themselves as they marched up the ramp to the palace and decided, *'Ramses will command these men one day, checking his ego here today may well mean life for them in some future battle.'*

Moses brought the defenders to a halt on the patio at the top of the ramp, saluted the general, bowed before Seti and reported, "General, I present to you the defenders you gave me command of. We have executed your orders. We returned to the village well before dark but found that the raiders had attacked earlier than ordered. We pursued them into the desert, devised a plan to draw them out of their hiding place, captured them, freed the villagers, and now present to you the raiders and their leader as you ordered."

Patie shuffled nervously glanced at Seti and said, "Well done Moses, congratulations to you and the defenders. You adapted well to the unexpected, followed your orders and accomplished your mission. But to be clear before the Pharaoh, I did not give orders permitting you to bind his royal Highness, and I regret your lack of discretion in bringing him before the Pharaoh and these witnesses in such a condition.

Seti, stood and moved forward to where Patie, Moses and the defenders stood. Moses dropped to his knees and the defenders followed suit.

"Stand Moses, you and your defenders." Seti motioned the captain of his guard forward and said, "Loose the crown prince."

Ramses jumped from the cart as the ropes were cut. "He held his hands up before his father and said, "See how the ropes have cut into my flesh, father. I commanded Moses to take the ropes off me and he refused my command and did so in front of these men. I demand that he be charged with treason, with harming the person of a member of the royal family, and that these men who witnessed and participated in his treasonous acts be punished."

Seti rubbed his face, sighed and said, "You will not address me as father in this setting. I am your Pharoah. Now, do not speak again."

Turning to the assembled troops he said, "You and each of you, Raiders and defenders alike, are to be congratulated on the completion of this exercise. Each of you have my pledge that none will be punished for their actions therein. Now, leave us."

Once the troops had departed Seti said, "General Patie, Moses, and Ramses follow me to the court chamber, where you will make a full report to me and the members of my court."

Chapter Nine

The Decision

The wind shifted in the early morning, enabling it to slip past the screen surrounding the couch on which Moses lay. The breeze chilled the flesh on his exposed shoulder and snaked down his back, pulling him from the deep darkness of early morning sleep. Moses sat up, rubbed the sleep from his eyes, and sat thinking about his dream. He rubbed a hand across his chin and reviewed the scene before Seti and his court during the report Seti had demanded.

The General explained how he had planned the exercise, the building of the 'village,' the division of the class into those who would raid and those who would defend. He explained that he placed Ramses and Moses in command of the groups because they were senior due to their status as royalty. He repeated his orders that sent Moses and the defenders on patrol and instructed Ramses and the defenders to attack after dark. He carefully but thoroughly explained that Ramses attacked early and that once Moses and the defenders set out in pursuit of the raiders, he had returned to the palace to await the victor.

Seti asked, "Why did you not stop the exercise once you saw that Ramses had struck early?"

Moses remembered thinking, 'Interestingly, grandfather avoided saying that Ramses disobeyed the General's orders.'

Patie responded, "Because Highness, my thought was, this will be a chance to see how Moses would react in this real-world circumstance where things do not always go as planned."

Moses remembered several members of the court nodding their heads and some expressing their agreement with the General.

Seti frowned at the members who were divided in support of Ramses and Moses. After order was restored, Seti asked Patie, "General, did you give any additional instructions to Moses?"

"No, Pharoah, I did not."

"I see, Moses, you said that you lured Ramses out of his hiding place. Three questions for you, first, where was the hiding place, how did you know where to find him, and how did you lure him out?"

Moses paused, thinking through his answer before speaking, *'Do I tell Pharoah that Ramses crossed the border violating the General's orders for a second time? Or do I shield Ramses with an answer that is less than the total truth?'*

Pharaoh spoke, "Moses, I see the struggle on your face. I warn you that I am speaking to you as your Pharaoh, not your grandfather. Lie to me, and it will not go well with you."

Ramses spoke, saying, "Please forgive my interruption Pharaoh, may I answer that question since the answer involves my command decisions in the exercise?"

Seti nodded his consent.

Ramses continued, "I confess that I made a command decision to create a more realistic test of Moses' command ability. I did so by striking the target earlier than he anticipated. I led my raiders across the border into a ravine between two watchtowers. I knew that the General had ordered us not to cross the border to avoid a problem with the Ethiopians. But, I also knew that using the cover of darkness and stealth, I could remain out of sight in the ravine, and being located equal distance between the towers, I would be alerted should either group of guards discover our presence. I knew we could exit the gully and cross the border back into Egypt before the reaction force could reach us, avoiding any incident with the Ethiopians.

I knew Moses had patrolled the border, and chances were that he had seen the ravine and would know that I might choose it as a hiding place, but I thought he would be too timid to cross the border to flush me out.

So, yes, I disobeyed the General and crossed the border. But as I had calculated, I was able to exit the ravine and cross the border quickly once I saw the signal lantern hoisted on the first watchtower.

And I would have been able to escape and return to the palace the victor except that Moses had anticipated my move and had his men lying in wait for me."

Once again, the court members murmured as they understood the plan Moses had developed and executed. Seti barked, "Quiet." And the members fell silent though a couple of them pointed at Moses and gave him a thumbs up.

"Do you have anything else to say?" Seti asked

"Only this Pharaoh, I withdraw my charge of treason against Moses. I congratulate him on his victory, and I apologize to the General for taking liberty with his orders."

Seti nodded and said, "Good, thank you for the humility; it is a trait you need to exercise more often. General, I command you to record Moses and his defenders as having shown themselves qualified for active duty in the ready reserve. Moses has demonstrated he is ready for command, and his defenders have shown themselves ready for action. Ramses needs more training in command situations. His raiders should remain in training also."

There was a smattering of laughter from the members of the court. "Enough!" shouted Seti. "All of you will do well to remember that your mirth is at the expense of your next Pharaoh. You will leave our presence now. General, you go with them. Moses and Ramses, you remain.

Moses grimaced as he recalled his grandfather's next words, "My heartaches. The two of you could combine to lead Egypt in the domination of the world if you would put this animosity aside and each see the value of the other. But I fear you will not. Rather, your differences will lead to one destroying the other once I am gone. Moses, you can leave now; I wish to speak with the crown prince in private."

Moses bowed before his grandfather and backed out of the chamber. One outside the door, he stepped away then turned back and stood listening to the Pharoah speak, "Ramses, I am sorely disappointed in you, my son. Your jealousy of Moses is unfounded. He is a Hebrew and will never reign; that is yours by birthright, and I have secured the vote of enough members of the court to ensure your accession to the throne once I am gone. Put this useless rivalry aside and see Moses for what he is, an asset to assist you in your rule."

"Father, I do not like Moses; I do not trust Moses. Moses has a trait that you are not aware of; he always thinks he has a better idea. He tends to allow that belief to lead him into spontaneous actions contrary to what he has been told. I know this sounds strange coming from me given my disobedience of the General's orders, but I know that I could never trust him to obey me. He will never be a member of my court. I intend to drive him away, if possible, to have him leave Egypt."

Moses felt faint, 'He intends to drive me out; I will be a stateless person. It seems that my lot does indeed lie with the Hebrews. There is no need to wait; Ramses has made the decision for me; I will cast my lot with my people."

Chapter ten

Three Hebrew Brothers

Moses lifted his arms over his head, stretched to the right then to the left, trying to clear his head. He reached for his robe and stood.

He wrapped the robe around him and slipped his sandals on. He heard voices raised in argument and strolled from his sleeping quarters onto the patio overlooking the Nile. The speakers were shielded from his view by the screens set up to protect the royal family from the view of those who walked along the patio. But the still quietness of the early morning allowed Moses to hear what was being said, "Listen to me, Remy. I was in the palace; I had slipped in to visit Mira while the queen was in her bath. We were hidden in an alcove when Moses and Ramses came in.

We were not twenty feet from where they stood arguing. I heard Moses tell Ramses that we were valuable to Egypt and that he should treat us better. I heard Ramses tell Moses we were slaves, that he would soon be our master, and that he would use us as it pleased him.

I also heard him tell Moses that he would never rule in Egypt because he was not Egyptian but Hebrew. I heard him refer to Moses being drawn from the Nile, just as our fathers have told. Remy, it is not a legend. It is true; Moses is one of us. He is Hebrew."

"You cannot believe that, Jacob. But even if it were true, what has Moses ever done for us? Nothing. And by your own words, you say that Moses will never rule in Egypt, so what can he do for us? Nothing. Why put your hope in this man, an emasculated prince of our enemy?

"Listen to you. You do not have a Hebrew name, your name, Remy, comes from the Egyptian culture, not the Hebrew. But none of us believe that you are our enemy.

Your family has found favor within the palace and enjoys the fruit of that favor in housing, clothing, food, and exemption from the slave labor details. How many bricks have you made, Remy? Never mind, I know the answer to that. Your flesh is pasty white from spending your days in the shade of the palace. Look at your hands; how soft they are. They have never known a day's work. The only calluses I see are those on your knees. You got those from crawling before the royalty, begging for scraps from their table. You are not a Hebrew; you are an amusement, a clown for the entertainment of our captors."

"I am more Hebrew than you ever will be. My heritage is of Dan; yours is of what, Manasseh? My heritage is that of warriors, yours of a feeble few. You have insulted me; follow me down by the river, and we will see who is the better Hebrew."

Moses shrugged out of his robe and ran down the steps. A gust of morning breeze parted the morning fog, and he saw the two Hebrews standing with fists clenched, red of face, and ready to fight. They turned toward the Nile, and Moses called out, "Hold. Stay where you are. What is this? Are two Hebrews willing to fight over who is more Hebrew? One will destroy the other, and our cause is weakened. Why serve the enemy? Stand together like brothers against the common enemy."

"Easy for you to say. Your life has been one of ease and privilege since the day you were drawn from the Nile. You are by law, a prince of Egypt; why should we listen to you? You are our enemy."

"No, I am not Remy. I am Hebrew. I heard your argument. You are of Dan; Jacob is of Manasseh. Me, I am of Levi. Three, each from different tribes, but the same heritage. We are Hebrews all three heirs of the covenant. True, you and I have not been in the field laboring as Jacob and his have. But we are just as much captive as he is. This is what I purpose.

Pharaoh has endorsed to the court Ramses suggestion. I will be walking among our people. My presence should mitigate the harshness with which the guards treat our brothers. I will intervene when I see abuse. I want people to see me. I want them to come to expect me to be there with them in the field as they labor. You, Jacob, continue to tell what you heard and tell it with the same passion you said to Remy. Please spread the word; Moses is a Hebrew, Moses is for us, change is coming.

As for you, Remy, you come out of the palace and walk among the people, share in the labor as much as your palace duties will allow. Let the people become comfortable with your presence; let them identify with you. When the time comes to rise, I will need help, especially in winning the people we will lead. Agreed?"

"Agreed," shouted Jacob. "I am in, and I will spread the word."

"So, the Hebrew Prince of Egypt is going to leave the comfort of the palace, the royal family, to mix with the common folks? I am going to join in to see how long this lasts; it should be interesting to watch the one taken from captivity forty years ago step back into the slave mentality."

"Ah, you miss the point, Remy. My goal is to free the people from the slave mentality; I want your help. That change in how they see themselves is necessary to give them a vision of freedom."

"One last thing; remember the Pharaoh's order that any Hebrews found fighting or harming another Hebrew will be punished by transport to the mines in the north. Temper your passions so we can work together and lead our people out of captivity, agreed?"

Remy nodded and walked up the slope toward the palace. Jacob turned to join the crew cleaning up around the patio of the palace.

Moses returned to the palace for breakfast with his adoptive mother. His chin dropped onto his chest as he trudged up the slope thinking, *'I did as she suggested, I reviewed the exercise and the follow-up as we reported to grandfather. The memory of what I overheard has convinced me that I have no future with Egypt. How will I tell her that I am leaving the royal family and returning to my people? I do not want to hurt her, but the time has come for me to return to my roots.*

****

Moses allowed his emotions free reign as he lingered over his breakfast. *'I will miss this place, the beauty, the ease of life for one who is a member of the royal family.'*

He fidgeted in his chair as he recalled the tension between him and Hatsheput following their appearance before Seti. They had discussed his assignment to walk among the Hebrews to observe them and their Egyptian masters in the daily labors. She had pleaded with him to not let his concern for the abuse of the slaves lead him into an injudicious action. He recalled his response, "Mother, I will not stand idly by and allow my brother Hebrew be beaten by a guard when I can stop it. I will order it stopped in the name of pharaoh."

"No, Moses. Please don't do it. This is part of Ramses plan to move you out of the royal family, to have you seen by the court as a Hebrew more than an Egyptian. Wait, time heals all things, let the tension between you and Ramses have time to lessen, the heat of summer is about to give way to fall, then winter will come and with it a slowing of the workload on the Hebrews. The overseers do not like to take the crews out in the winter weather so the opportunity for you to walk among them daily will not be there.

Stay visible to father and your supporters within the cabinet. Go to court each day; find ways to serve. Let the other members of the court identify you with service to the realm."

Then when spring comes you will see things differently, you will have more options. Do this for me please Moses, don't break your mother's heart with a rash decision.

Moses hesitated. 'I should honor her request,' he thought. But then, he faced the truth; deep down he knew that it was the fear of the unknown, of moving from this life of luxury as a member of the royal family into the life of those in bondage that was the cause of his hesitation. She moved to him, laid her head on his shoulder, put her arms around him and sobbed, “You are my life, I can feel the pull of your heritage on you, but you must wait; take your time in making such an important decision; you must consider both your legacy and your lineage. The right decision at the wrong time can be disastrous for both.”

Moses made the decision in that instant, with the mention of his lineage. That was the deciding factor, his lineage, ‘*my people had endured enough, the right decision for me is to lead them out of bondage, and the time is now.’*

"I cannot do that, mother. To do so would be to deny my lineage. I am Hebrew; I belong with my people.

"Then stop calling me, mother! Go if you must but go knowing that you have broken my heart."

Moses pushed away from the table and moved down the stairs from the marble floors into the Egyptian dust.

He heard the rhythmic call of pull, pull, pull. He turned toward the sound and saw one of the flatbottomed scows used to transport materials along the Nile approaching. He heard the Helmsman say, "rest and watched as the heavy craft slowed and then stopped.

The Helmsman raised his voice once again to say, "Starboard bank rest easy, port bank, pull on my command to turn her into the wharf, now, pull you lazy Hebrews, pull." Moses winced as he heard the crack of a whip followed by the cry of the one it had been directed to. The nose of the craft swung toward the bank, and the Helmsman barked, "all together now, pull, pull, now all back."

The craft slowed and came to rest in the slip cut next to the warf. Moses walked toward the scow, and the Helmsman saw him, "Good morning, Highness. What can I do for you?"

"Nothing, Pharaoh asked me to observe the Hebrews and our oversight of them in their daily labors. I will watch you unload and then move on to observe more. Go about your business as if I am not here."

The Helmsman nodded and then turned to the crew. Get these bricks off the scow and onto those skids you see hooked to the oxen. Hurry, there is a storm building in the east and I want to get these unfired bricks under cover before the rain falls. Rain will ruin those unfired bricks. Careful now; they are very fragile. I will have a pound of Hebrew flesh for every brick that is broken."

Moses watched as one group of slaves began to carry bricks to wheelbarrows which other slaves then moved to the skids where a third group of slaves unloaded the wheelbarrows, stacking the bricks on the skids.

Moses followed the first group of skids toward the kiln to observe the bricks' unloading and firing. He stood watching the activity. He saw that the work gang here at the kiln was supervised by a Hebrew who took directions from an Egyptian overseer watching from a tower built at the corner of the kiln. A lightning bolt raced across the darkening skies, followed by the crash of thunder, and a few heavy drops of rain fell.

"Hurry, you fools, get this load into the kiln before the skies open. Hebrew, send one of those men to the river and tell the Helmsman to cover the bricks with a tarp and wait until this storm passes before, he unloads anymore."

Moses saw the Hebrew overseer pull one of the slaves out of line and push him toward the Nile. The messenger ran toward the river, and Moses followed. Halfway to the river, the skies opened, and a wall of water cut the visibility to a few feet in any direction. Moses pushed on through the rain and saw the messenger on his knees seeking cover under a small tree. A movement to his right caught Moses's attention. He saw an Egyptian soldier approaching the kneeling Hebrew. Moses could see the Egyptian was yelling something at the Hebrew, but he could not hear what he was saying because of the howling wind. Moses moved forward slowly and heard, "So, you thought you would use the storm to run away and hide, did you?"

The slave started to stand, pointed toward the river, and said, "No, master. I was sent to carry a message to the Helmsman of the scow jut there."

The Egyptian was advancing on the slave now in a trot; Moses saw him remove a whip from his belt and heard him say, "On your knees, Hebrew, stay on your knees."

The slave kneeled, and the Egyptian lifted the whip, and Moses saw it snake out toward the kneeling slave. It struck the slave And then again. Moses moved forward, and the Egyptian saw him in his peripheral vision. He turned toward Moses and lifted the whip. As he was about to send the whip toward Moses, he recognized who his target was. He hesitated and dropped the whip.

Moses could not speak. There was a roaring in his ears, and his throat was tight. His anger pushed him forward until he stood before the Egyptian. Moses turned to the slave and stuttered, "continue your mission."

The slave stumbled away toward the river. Moses turned to the Egyptian and managed to say, "You had no right to beat that man."

"Man? That was no man; you stuttering fool. That was a Hebrew slave. I know you are partial to the slaves, seeing as how you are one of them, but I am a soldier of the realm and here in the field, I may do as I think necessary to maintain discipline among them."

Moses did not hear the rest of what the soldier said, he lashed out, striking the soldier in the throat with his closed fist. All his frustration and anger were unleashed in that single blow. The Egyptian fell to his knees and then onto his face. Moses knelt beside him and turned him onto his back. The Egyptian was struggling to breathe. A gurgling whistle came from his throat and then a thin trickle of blood from his mouth. Moses knew that he has crushed the windpipe and that the soldier was drowning in his blood. As he kneeled there watching the Egyptian die, he heard Ramses words echoing in his mind, *"your intemperate passion will prevent you from realizing your promise."*

Moses grabbed the Egyptians' feet and dragged him behind the little tree to a sand dune. He broke through the top layer of sand, crusted now by the rain, scooped out a hollow, and rolled the Egyptian into it. He pulled the sand from the top of the dune into the hollow covering the body. Moses shuffled around, covering his tracks as much as possible in the tacky sand. Satisfied that he had covered his tracks, he returned to the kiln. As he approached, he saw the guards and the slaves huddled together seeking shelter from the wind driven rain on the far side of the building. *'If I can sneak in among them, they will think that I have been here with them this entire time.'* he thought.

Moses slowed his pace and crept along the front of the building to the corner nearest where the group stood. One of the guards sensed his presence and looked at him, the guard pushed a slave away from the building and stepped aside saying, "Your wet Majesty, step in here out of the rain."

Moses moved into the vacated space and said, "Thank you. The wind lifted a corner of the tarp, and I took time to pull it back into place to protect the bricks.

The guard leaned away from the building and peeped at the pallet of bricks that Moses pointed at. He smiled and said, "Thank you majesty, you have saved me from the wrath of the overseer. He would not have been happy if those brick had melted in this storm."

Chapter Eleven

The Body of Evidence

There was one last gust of wind, and the rain stopped as suddenly as it had started. The guards stepped away from the building and removed their whips from their belts. The camaraderie of men huddled together seeking shelter from a common peril was gone as quickly as the storm. The slaves moved to the pallets, anxious to avoid the pain of being struck.

Moses watched for a minute and then moved to the overseer. "You are doing an excellent job, the site is well organized, and the work proceeds at the perfect pace. My report to pharaoh will include a recommendation that you be cited for your performance."

"Thank you, majesty."

Moses nodded and said, “where do I go to see the bricks being molded?"

The overseer pointed to the Northeast and said, "I will send one of my men with your majesty. It is not safe for a prince of Egypt to be alone and unarmed amid these Hebrews."

Moses cast a quick look at his belt and said, "I did not think about arming myself this morning. Pharaoh's instructions to me were to walk among the slaves and their overseers to observe and report to him how the work progresses and the mood among the slaves. He has heard that there is discontent brewing because our hand has been a bit heavy of late. He does not want an insurrection among the Hebrews.

I don't feel threatened; you and your men have these Hebrews well subdued. I will find my way, keep your man here to help you accomplish your task."

Moses patted the overseer on the shoulder and walked away to the Northeast as if headed to inspect the bricks' production. He stopped on the crest of the first dune and looked back toward the kiln; it was no longer possible to see anything save the chimney and the thin trail of smoke rising from the fire inside.

Moses walked down the slope of the dune and turned back toward the Nile. On level ground, he looked up and could not see over the top of the dune. Bending at the waist, he raced toward that spot where he had left the body of the Egyptian.

He saw the small tree and turned to the dune where the body was buried. He gasped at the sight of two booted feet sticking out from the base of the dune. He stuttered, *'The storm uncovered him.'*

Moses knelt before the feet and pulled sand down from the dune to cover them. The sun had dried the sand, and the crust formed from the rain had given way to soft grains of sand that were carried away by the light breeze as Moses tried to cover the dead Egyptian. Realizing that his efforts were in vain, Moses moved a few feet to the right of the body and began to scoop out a deeper grave into the dune. Satisfied, he rolled the dead Egyptian into the grave and set about pulling sand over him. He covered the body from the feet up, and as he pulled sand down to cover the face, he realized the Egyptian had died with a grimace that resembled a smile on his face. Moses winced, thinking, *'He is smiling at me, telling me that his body will be the evidence that brings me down.'*

Moses shook his head, trying to displace the thought. He pulled more sand down and over the face, then added another layer to it. He pushed up from his knees, broke a limb from the small tree, and used it to sweep away his tracks. *'If only I could sweep away this body of evidence,'* he thought and walked away.

Moses climbed the steps to the patio outside his quarters and turned, looking to the Nile. His eyes drifted toward where he buried the body. As his eyes swept over the burial site, he realized that anyone standing in this elevated spot could have seen him as he buried the Egyptian. *'That means they could have seen me kill him,'* Moses felt a chill run up his back as he realized that he might have been seen.

He shrugged, turned toward his quarters, and a cooling bath, "Well, if it is not the prince of Egypt, never to be pharaoh."

Moses recognized the voice of Ramses and dopped to one knee; he bowed from the waist and said, "Good afternoon, crown prince. Yes, it is me, your humble and faithful servant returning from performing my duties as directed by you and pharaoh."

"Really? It appears you have been digging in the sand. How does that serve the realm?"

"Forgive me, my Lord. Pharaoh suggested to me that I walk among the Hebrews and the overseers to observe the work, the treatment of the slaves, and to report to your highness on the mood among the slaves."

"You have edited one statement in a long discussion to fit your goals, Moses. But I suppose it is a harmless endeavor and if it keeps you busy and out of my way, proceed."

"Thank you, pharaoh. Now with your leave, I will retire to my quarters and a bath to remove this sand and alleviate the itching.

"Yes, you may leave our presence, Moses. The bath will remove the sand, but the itch is from the fleas that nest in the sand. Their bite leaves a stinging that lingers for days. Much like the time I spend in your presence. Go now, so the healing can begin for us both."

Moses waited until Ramses had walked away, then stood. He walked into his quarters, called his attendant, and had him pour a bucket of cool water over his legs and feet and then to fill his tub with hot water. Moses stepped into his tub and sat letting the hot water open his pours. He ate a late supper and stretched out on his couch; his last thought before sleep overcame the itch was, "*Did anyone see me kill or bury the Egyptian?*

Chapter Twelve

Called out

The first rays of morning sneaked in through the slit high in the east wall of Moses' sleeping quarters. It fell directly across his eyes. The sunbeam was full of the heat that each dawn of summer promised.

Moses rolled to his left to escape the interloper. The sunbeam now found the nape of his neck, quickly becoming uncomfortable. Moses sighed, sat up, and stood to face the day. He glanced at the sun pouring through the slit and thought, *"Okay, so you have me up, now what will you bring me today*?"

He washed his face in cool water and chose a light-colored, loose-fitting top and bottom combination for the day. *"This is better suited for my day in the hot sun,'* he reasoned. He pulled the bell cord, walked to the patio, and sat at his table waiting for the servants to bring his breakfast.

Moses ate slowly, then lingered over a cup of tea. He started to rise but sat back. *'Someone saw me; I can feel it in my spirit.'*

Moses went back to his sleeping quarters and changed from the light clothing into heavier clothing. He replaced his sandals with boots, added a turban for his head, strapped a heavy belt with his short sword around his waist, and turned to leave. He saw a rod, a long walking stick really, leaning in the corner and on impulse grabbed it. As he walked from his quarters and down the steps, he paused and looked back at the palace and found himself thinking, *'Will I ever be back, when will I see mother again?"* AS he walked away, he heard in his spirit, *'Yes, but you will come as an heir to the promise, not as a Prince of Egypt.'*

Moses decided to check the burial site of the Egyptian. As he approached the grave, he heard voices raised in anger, "No, it is your turn. I drew the water and loaded it on the skid, yesterday. Today it is yours to do. Today it is my turn to drive the oxen and ride the skid."

Moses walked on and saw the two who were arguing. As he approached, he saw one standing on the water skid and the second one push him from his perch and step onto the skid.

The dislodged Hebrew was enraged and charged His assailant, striking him in the face with his closed hand. The fight was on, with the combatants exchanging blow for blow. Moses saw blood coming from the nose of the smaller of the two.

Moses ran to the fight and pushed the larger man away from his smaller victim. "Why do you bully your brother? In doing so, you become his oppressor the same as the Egyptians."

The smaller man recognized Moses and bowed, saying, "Forgive us, highness, we are brothers, we will stop fighting and get back to work."

Moses glanced at the bigger man and said, "My brother, violence is never the answer to a disagreement. Stop and reason with each other. Why would you demand an unequal division of labor between you and this man? Why put the heavier burden on your smaller and, I suspect, younger brother? It appears that you bear the greater wrong here."

The larger brother smirked at Moses and said, "Brother, you say? He and I are brothers, born of the same womb. But you are not our brother. You may well have Hebrew blood, but you chose the Egyptians over us when you allowed the queen to claim you as a son. That was your choice in life; we have little choice concerning our life. But we do have the option of who we allow to judge us. And we ask, who appointed you to be that judge?

You speak of violence, never being the answer? Why did you then turn to violence yesterday when you saw the Egyptian beating the Hebrew who had sought shelter from the rain under the tree? I was standing on the patio, enjoying the cool

Refreshing rain, and saw you strike the Egyptian and watched as you buried him in the dune. Why did you not reason with him, Moses?"

Moses felt his chest tighten as he realized that not only had this Hebrew witnessed him kill the Egyptian, but that he was calling him out on it. Seti would know by the end of the day. He realized why he had been moved to change into the heavier clothing. He knew that he must flee or face death at the hand of the pharaoh.

But which way to go? Gaining control of his emotions, Moses knew that his only option was to flee to the most desolate area if he was to escape the pharaohs' hand. *"Midian, I will go to Midian."* he found himself saying as he walked away from the mocking voice of the Hebrew bully. "Run, Moses, run. Seti will be after you before the moon rises tonight.

Chapter Thirteen

The Oasis

Moses walked through the day and into the night. As the heat of the day gave way to the chill of the desert night, he was thankful that he had dressed in heavy clothing that morning. He was especially grateful for his heavy boots that protected his feet from the sharp stones, thorns, and scorpions he had encountered during his race out of Egypt.

Now, he watched the sunrise in the east and adjusted his route to keep in a southeasterly direction. He climbed a small hill and saw a valley before him. The sun was already high, and the heavy clothing that had been so welcome in the night chill now became heavy and hot.

"I cannot travel during the day; the heat will kill me. And besides that, I cannot chance any traveler seeing me and reporting my route to the pharaoh. I will find shelter in that valley below, rest through the day and be ready to travel tonight. Midian is in the Northeast corner of Arabia. It should take me no more than eight days to walk there.

His decision was made, Moses walked down the hill and into a grove of trees next to a stream. He noticed that the stream was running in a southeasterly direction and appeared to run the valley's length. Moses turned to his left and walked north upstream to find its source; he heard it before seeing it, a jet of water spewing from the ground from an opening partially hidden by two large stones. The jetting stream pooled in a gravel lined depression and trickled through the small rocks to flow downstream. Moses leaned forward and reached his hand into the water at the point it left the ground. It was cold. He cupped his hand, let it fill with the cold clear water, and took a drink. There was a slight musky odor and taste. He spewed the water out and moved down below the graveled pool. He knelt and smelled the water there. There was no musky odor; he tasted it and found it sweet, light, and free of the musky taste. *'Ah, the gravel has filtered the impurities out,'* he thought.

Moses lay flat and drank his fill. He rose and moved downstream to the grove of trees; further downstream, he saw what he thought were date trees. 'Could it be?', he wondered, 'Could this be a small oasis here in the desert?' A chill ran through his heart as he realized that if so, travelers would know, and he ran the risk of being discovered.

Still, he was hungry. Moses hurried to the grove, collected enough dates to fill him, and then moved back upstream. He wedged himself in behind the stones covering the opening of the stream. It was perfect, he was out of the sun, and the water spewing from deep within the earth cooled the air around him. He ate, stretched out, and slept.

Chapter Fourteen

The Caravan

Moses woke. His senses had alerted him to a change; he lay still, focusing on that alert. Was there a threat? No, he did not feel threatened, but he felt a need to remain unseen.

Moses rolled onto his side and squirmed his way to the opening between the boulders forming the screening wall for his lair. He smelled the pungent odor of camels on the breeze flowing in from the desert. Now he could hear voices, they were faint, and he could tell that those he was hearing had not yet entered the Oasis. Moses lifted himself to one knee and peered around the boulder. Shadows of men and their animals moved along the edge of the Oasis and entered downstream from where he lay. He watched as the camels were led to drink, then staked out away from the stream so as not to foul it. The men rolled out blankets and lay down beside their animals. Quiet soon returned to the Oasis. Moses watched for a while, then he too lay down, and slept again.

Moses woke to the sound of the caravan moving out of the Oasis to continue their journey. Moses could see the men and their animals more clearly in the morning light. He listened to their chatter and recognized their accent, '*These men are from Midian,*' he realized.

He watched as the caravan moved away from the Oasis. *They will know the quickest, best route to Midian; I will wait until dark and follow them, their tracks will be easily seen in the moonlight,*' he decided.

The shaded glen in which Moses lay was cool; he had water and food within reach. He slept, building his strength for the nights' journey that lay in front of him.

As the sun set and the heat of the day waned, Moses rose, gathered his cloak about him, and stepped out of his Oasis. The caravan's track was as easy to find as he had anticipated, and he could see that they were indeed headed for Midian. The ground was smooth, and Moses made good time.

Moses became aware that the eastern sky was showing the first pink glow of the coming day. He could see the caravans' tracks more clearly. Ahead of him was a shallow depression, *'what do the nomads call these? A wadi, that's it, a wadi.'* he mumbled. A camel brayed, and Moses knew the animal had smelled him. He knew that the night guards would be looking to see what the camel was braying at. He hurried to the wadi and slid down the bank. Small bushes filled the bottom of the depression. Moses saw one large enough to offer full concealment and crawled under it. Soon, he heard the crunch of the night guards as they walked along the upper rim. Moses lay still until he heard the caravan breaking night camp and moving on. Comfortable that it was safe for him to emerge from concealment, he climbed the bank and saw that the caravan was already fading from sight. A hot wave of the morning air whistled across the desert, stinging Moses with sand. He returned to his bush and, using his hands, scooped the sand away from the plant's base. Soon the dry sand became moist, and then water began to fill the little hole. Moses let it fill and then lay on his belly and drank the gritty but refreshing water. He lay in the shade until fatigue overcame his hunger pangs, he slept through the heat of the day sheltered at the bottom of the wadi. Now, hunger pangs overcame his sleep, and he woke in the darkness. He scooped deeper into the sand around his bush and drank his fill again. Moses climbed out of the wadi and continued his journey.

Chapter 15

Journey's End

The darkest part of the night passed. The new day came breaking through. Moses heard men and animals, lifted his face into the breeze, and caught the smell of camels.

"*They are close. I will see them from the top of that next dune,*' he thought.

Moses climbed the dune, and there lay the camp before him. The men caught sight of him and raised the alarm. Moses lifted his arms and showed the men that his hands were empty.

One of the men stepped forward and called to Moses, "Good morning, Moses, come take bread and water with us."

Moses made a quick decision to answer truthfully, "thank you, I am out of Egypt, and my destination is Midian. I was in the oasis where you spent the night, I heard you talking and recognized your accent as those of Midian. I followed your caravan thinking you would know the quickest route to Midian. I am curious, how did you know my name?"

"I knew who you were as soon as I saw you enter our camp. Pharaoh's men stopped and inspected our caravan, as we were leaving Egypt; they were looking for you. The officer in charge offered us gold for information concerning you and warned that Pharaoh had decreed death for anyone found hiding you or facilitating your escape. He said you killed one of Pharaoh's soldiers. Is that so, Moses?"

"Yes, I intervened when I found him beating a Hebrew slave. We fought, and I killed him. I knew Pharaoh would be looking for me, so I am fleeing to Midian, where I believe I will be out of his reach or at least can lose myself in the wilderness. But now, tell me. Are you going to take me to Pharaoh for the reward or to avoid his wrath?"

"The short answer to your question is no. But let me correct you when you say we are Midianites. We prefer to think of ourselves as Cush who live in Midian. Let me ask you this, Moses, do you know the history of the Cush who became the Ethiopians and then Midianites?

"No, I did not know that the Midianites emanated from the Ethiopians or Cush."

"We did, those of us living in the south of Ethiopia were called Cush. We moved to the north and over time there was intermarriage between us. We sought to become one people with them, but there was a prejudice against those of us with dark skin. The children born of the intermarriages were usually dark skinned. Why, I don't know, perhaps our blood is stronger.

But there was tension as those of us with dark skin became the majority. Over time the light skinned began to speak against intermarriage, denied us equal opportunity to own land and flocks, they seized our property and the wealth we had accumulated while in their service. Then they began to sell us to the Midianite traders who operate the caravans. The Midianites valued our women for their skill as shepherdesses. We were more welcome with them than with the Ethiopians and over time we aligned with them. That is how we came to be known as Midianites, but in our hearts, we are still the Cush.

The Ethiopians see us as traitors for uniting with their enemy, the Midianites.

Moses nodded his thanks and turned to continue his journey. "Wait, Moses, are you hungry? Do you thirst?"

"Yes, but I see a well in the distance. I intend to sit there, slake my thirst, and wait to see who comes during the day. I have prayed to my God, Yahweh, and I believe he will bring me those I am to align with here in Midian.

Aeriel stepped forward, clasped Moses's hand, and said, "Moses, the well you speak of belongs to the Kenite clan of Midian. My brother Reuel is their chief priest. You will hear his people call him Jethro, don't be confused. His birth name is Reuel, which means friend of God, but his people call him Jethro because it means excellence, overflow, or abundance.

I tell you Moses, we Midianites of the Cush value loyalty in a man. We have heard of your loyalty to your blood. Remain loyal to us, and you and yours will have friends and allies, leave us, betray our hospitality and protection, and we will become your people's bitter enemies."

Moses nodded and moved to the shaded side of the well. He sat, leaning his back against the cool stone, and thought about what Aeriel had said, *"Don't leave or betray us. Does that mean that if I do not stay with the Midianites as long as I live that they will see my leaving as betrayal and become the enemy of my people?"* He shook his head and thought, *"one day at a time Moses, one day at a time."* He leaned his head back against the well and slept.

Chapter Sixteen

Zipporah

Moses was dreaming of the Egyptian, the look on his dead face as the sand was scooped over him. He was drawn into consciousness by the sound of voices. He had slumped during his sleep and his head was hanging below his center mass. There was a pressure on his eyes causing pain, his face and neck were hot, and there was a roaring in his head. Pushing against the sand, Moses forced himself into an upright position with his back firmly against the well. He sat still until his blood pressure normalized, his pulse slowed, the roaring in his head subsided and his vision cleared. He was surprised to see that the sun was dipping low in the western sky; he had slept all day. The voices drew nearer, and Moses focused trying to understand what the people were saying.

The voices were drawing closer; he leaned in to try and sort out how many different voices he was hearing. Moses counted each different voice, '*there are seven of them all women,'* thought. Moses stood and turned to face the voices.

He startled the women, and they turned to run. "Wait, I mean you no harm. My name is Moses, I am an Egyptian. I came in from the desert and sat down to rest. Without meaning to, I slept the day away. Your voices awakened me just now.

Come, I will help you draw your water, and maybe you have a crust of bread for me."

The women were hesitant, all except one. She was tall, thin, and very dark-skinned. She appeared to be the older of the seven. She stepped forward and said, "We have come to draw water for our father's flock. The troughs are there," she said, pointing to an enclosure of rough brush and limbs.

"The troughs are deep, and it takes a lot of effort to draw the water, carrying it to the troughs and fill them. It will take a an hour to meet the needs of the flock. We would appreciate a strong mans' help." She paused and looked at the at the other women. They laughed and nodded. Moses pushed the bucket into the well and waited until it the water far below. He tested the rope and when the bucket was heavy enough to be full, he drew it from the well. He sat the bucket down. The tall one grabbed it and walked toward the troughs. Another of the women stepped forward and handed Moses an empty bucket; he filled it and sat it on the well for her to carry away. She looked at Moses and said, "My sister likes you, Moses; I can tell. Her name is Zipporah."

"Hush, Rachel, I can speak for myself."

Moses looked up, uncomfortable by the comment made by the younger sister and that Zipporah had heard it."

He was made more uncomfortable by the direct frankness in Zipporah's eyes. She held his eyes with a message that caused him to flush and caused his tongue to cling to the roof of his mouth. He realized that his heart was pounding, and he could hear each beat in his ears. He stood there shivering in a cold sweat, unable to speak or to look away from those captivating eyes.

Zipporah pointed to the freshly filled bucket and said, "Rachel, take that to the trough; be careful not to spill any."

Rachel giggled, grabbed the bucket, and walked away, casting a look over her shoulder. "Go, Rachel, and mind your business, do not spill the water. And tell the others to stay at the trough until I call them," Zipporah scolded.

Moses knew that his life was about to change, change even more than when he chose to leave the royal family to live as a Hebrew. He swallowed and waited nervously as Zipporah walked around the well and laid her hand on his arm. "So, here we are Moses, you and I meeting at a well on the back

side of the desert. You know, this cannot be by chance. We are meant to be. I am forty years old and feared that
I had missed my chance to be a wife and mother, but the Lord gave me a dream last night that my life would be well watered and fruitful. I am a virgin Moses, created and preserved for you before there was time. It is ordained for us to be a couple."

She turned and called to her sisters, "Come, join us here at the well and let me tell you what has happened and what is going to happen."

****

Moses felt weak; his legs were shaking. He leaned against the wall for support. Zipporah noticed and said, "Stand up straight, I want my sisters to see the strong man that the Lord has sent me. And relax, take your time so you do not stutter."

Moses stood erect. The sister came running to the well. Rachel said to the others, "See, I told you that she had claimed him."

"Shush Rachel, now all of you sit and let me tell you."

Before Zipporah could get them settled, a group of herdsmen drove the flock into the enclosure. The lead herdsman called to the sisters, "Draw water to refresh my men. Bring them cups to drink from and then bring towels to wash the dust from them."

Zipporah stood, faced the man, and said, "We are your masters' daughters, we are not your handmaidens, draw water if you are thirsty, wash if you wish to be clean."

The herdsman was angered, and it showed in his face, "You may be Reuel's daughters, but you are still women, and women will not speak like this to men. Now do as you are told, and we will let Reuel judge between us."

Moses stood and faced the man, "I will stand as the judge until Reuel can. You and your herdsmen leave, or I will indeed judge and execute the sentence on you."

The force of Moses' voice shook the man. He waved to his herdsmen, and they left saying, "It is evening; the flock needs watering, we leave that to you women."

Moses watched until the men were out of sight and then said, "You return to your father and report what has happened, I will stay and safeguard the flock."

Chapter 17

Moses Takes a Wife

Zipporah led the way to their camp. She walked to her fathers' tent.

"Shall we go in with you, Zipporah, or wait?" Rachel asked.

"Come in with me; father will want a full report to hear from each of us."

"Father, we are back safely," she called and stepped in under the open tent.

Ruel nodded but did not answer. "Did all go well? Is the flock watered and bedded down for the night?" he asked.

His gaze was fixed on Zipporah.

"Yes, the flock is watered and safely in the enclosure for the night. We did have a confrontation with the herdsmen. They demanded we serve them first, with water to drink and then to wash them before watering the flock."

"And did you?"

"You know Zipporah better than that, father. She put them in their place and reminded them that they were speaking to the daughters of their master." Rachel said.

"Father, there was an Egyptian at the well when we arrived. He supported us before the herdsmen. He is very tall and stoutly built, an imposing figure of a man, one might say. The herdsmen were intimidated and turned away, leaving us in peace." Zipporah said.

"His name is Moses. He is an imposing figure of a man, indeed father. He is light skinned, stutters when he talks and has stolen Zipporah's heart," Rachel said.

"Where is this Egyptian?" Reuel asked.

"We left him to safeguard the flock," Zipporah replied.

"And did your heart remain with him?" Reuel smiled at his daughter.

Zipporah blushed and remained silent.

"Go get him, bring him to my fire. Feed the man and let me get to know him."

"I will go get him, father," Rachel giggled.

"No, Zipporah will bring him," Reuel said.

Zipporah ran from the tent. She did not slow her pace until she reached the well. She saw Moses sitting at the gate to the enclosure and said, "Come, father wants to meet you."

Moses rose and said, "What about the flock? We cannot leave them here unattended."

Zipporah laughed and said, "You have never attended a flock, have you? I noticed your hands also, they are soft, not the hands of a working man or of a warrior. Who and what at you Moses?

Moses avoided the question and asked, "what about the flock?"

"See the one with the red cord and small bells around her neck? She is the leader. I will take the rope, you open the gate, and I will come out with her. The others will follow her." Zipporah said.

Moses walked beside Zipporah, and the flock followed them to camp. Zipporah led the bell sheep into an enclosure, and the others followed. She then took Moses by the hand and led him to her fathers' tent.

"Father, this is Moses," she said.

Reuel nodded but did not take his eyes from Moses. "Welcome, My brother sent me a messenger that there was a famous Egyptian Prince at my well. Is that you?

"Please pardon me, I do not know the proper way to address you, but yes, I am the one your brother spoke of. My name is Moses. I was born a Hebrew, adopted into the royal family and declared a prince of Egypt by Pharaoh. But I am not Egyptian, I am Hebrew, of the tribe of Levi."

"You may address me as father. Sit with me, Moses. I have questions. Bring the man some bread," he said to his daughters.

Turning to Moses, he said, "The story of your loyalty to your people and your flight out of Egypt has preceded you. You are welcome in our camp. We know pharaoh has put a death sentence on you and that there is a promise of gold for those who take you to him, kill you or tell him where you are. We will protect you, and you will be our ally if you are with us. Do you intend to stay with us, or will you wait until the pharaoh is dead and then return to claim your inheritance as a member of the royalty?

"I have no inheritance as an Egyptian. I am a Hebrew of the tribe of Levi. Any inheritance I have lies with my people, in the covenant God made with Abraham. I was thinking fate has brought me here, but Zipporah says she believes it was ordained before there was time. I do not know what that may entail, or for how long, but I find it interesting. I promise you this, while I am with you, I will not betray our trust, I will be loyal to you as the leader of this clan, and I will earn my keep. I do not know how I will be useful to you for my training is in the military arts."

"You will be useful by applying your military training. I have large flocks scattered all over this region; I need help in planning their care, in developing a plan to rotate the grazing, so we do not overgraze one area, how to let a pasture rest, we need more wells, we need to develop markets for their wool, and we need a breeding schedule. Then there is the constant conflict between my herdsmen and the neighboring clans. You You know how to plan, organize, and manage people. I need a man with those skills, Moses.

"Will there not be jealously from those who have served you for all the years before my arrival?"

"Yes, there would be. I will give you a small flock, a group of people to go with you, and send you to the backside of our region. You will be of our clan, but a new branch of it. We will bring you along slow. If I am right, your skills will win them over, and your promotion will be their idea.

Are you willing?"

Moses nodded, "I see the wisdom in that. I left Egypt with nothing; I will need basic provision to get started."

"I will give you more than a basic provision. You will have supplies sufficient for six months, and I will allow Zipporah to go with you. You will need a companion, Zipporah has my blessing to live as your wife, if she agrees, and I see from the smile on her face that she does.

Finish your bread, then go to the big enclosure, select four hundred sheep and separate them as yours. Take Zipporah with you, she will know which sheep to select.

You will leave with your flock, your wife, and my blessings at first light. Zipporah knows where I want you to take the flock; she will guide you."

Moses clasped the offered hand and said, "Agreed, I will do my best for you but let me ask you, am I free to govern this new branch of your clan? How about our worship?"

"Moses, we are Druze. We do acknowledge the existence of God; we don't name Him other than to say God. I know that as a Hebrew you worship one you call Yahweh. I also know that you observe high holy days, festivals, and such. We Druze do not, we believe that one should worship God every day, we focus on our philosophy of life recognizing that we are spiritual beings here on earth for a set time, that to receive the favor, protection, and blessings of God we must be honest, must work, we must be faithful to God, to family and to clan. We believe that we must be involved with and work for the good of our society.

If you keep these tenants of our faith, then you are free to worship your Yahweh. Is that acceptable with you?"

"Yes, it is. I must worship the Lord, my God, and the philosophy you describe will augment, not interfere with the practice of my faith."

"It is settled then; I am the high priest of the Druze in our clan, and you are the high priest of those who worship Yahweh in your branch of the clan."

Chapter Eighteen

Sunrise

Moses lay on a coarse blanket spread on a patch of lumpy ground inside Reuel's tent. Reuel demanded Moses sleep under his tent, within his reach, so there would be no question concerning his daughters' honor. Reuel made it clear to Moses within the hearing of his council of elders that even though he had given Zipporah to him for marriage, there would be no habitation as man and wife until they had established their branch of the clan in the backside of the desert.

Reuel lay some three feet away, and Moses could hear his snoring. The old man turned in his sleep onto his left side; the smell of his breath flowed across the narrow divide. Moses thought Reuel's breath smelled of cheese, garlic and the stewed lamb served for last nights' dinner. He gagged and turned onto his left side to escape it. As he did, a sharp stone dug into his upper arm. Moses turned again and lay on his back, then onto his right side, and finally sat up. He had not slept, and there was no use laying on the rough ground.

He rolled onto his knees and stood. The sound of his rising woke Reuel, and he asked, "Are you so anxious to be on your way that you cannot sleep?"

Moses thought better of telling him that the lumpy ground, together with his snoring and smelly breath, kept him awake; instead, he said, "I am anxious for the new beginning, father." Reuel grunted and turned away. He was snoring instantly. Moses walked from the tent and faced east. He could see the first weakening of the darks' hold on this new land.

The night watch guard saw Moses and ambled over to join him. Nodding toward the coming dawn, he said, "Good Morning, Moses. I am Joshua. The new sun is climbing the east slopes of the mountains and will soon reach the summit. With it comes new challenges and new opportunities. My wife, Sara, and I have been chosen to go with you. My wife will serve our new branch of the clan as the doula.

I am trained in animal husbandry. I will help you in the management of our flock's growth.

Moses looked at the man with a new interest, "Your wife is trained as a doula, and you are trained in Animal husbandry; I have not heard these terms before; explain them to me."

The man nodded and said, "animal husbandry is the Controlled cultivation, management, and production of domestic animals, in our case sheep, including improvement of the qualities considered desirable for food, wool, being resistant to disease and utility or work. This is done, of course through selective breeding."

"A doula is a woman who has training in supporting a pregnant woman during her labor and birth."

Moses smiled and said, "Then you both will be engaged in growing our clan."

Moses saw Joshua smile and watched the shadows of night leave his face. The sun had topped the mountain and its' warming light flooded down the slopes, across the valley and into the camp. Moses heard a step behind him and turned to see Reuel coming from the tent, "Sunrise," he bellowed.

Joshua replied, "Yes father, I was just telling Moses that with it comes new challenges and new opportunities. We are ready to face the one and harvest the other."

"Good. Speaking of harvesting an opportunity, here comes your first Moses,"

Moses looked where Reuel pointed and saw Zipporah walking toward him with a smile on her face. "Good morning father, good morning husband."

Moses reached for her outstretched hand but quickly drew back as he heard Reuel clear his throat, "Father, you said I could choose to be as his wife at sunrise, and it is SUNRISE, and I have chosen to be as his wife."

A small crowd had gathered in front of Reuel's tent, and the old man said, "I said that you could choose to be as his wife once you reach your destination. You are part of his provision I am giving him to sustain him as he establishes this new branch of our clan. Here, he is still a guest, partaker of my hospitality, and subject to my house."

Zipporah was exasperated, "Father! I am not a commodity to be sent off to sustain this man while he establishes this new work. I am to be his partner, his help mate, and yes his wife."

Reuel shrugged and asked, "Moses, I know you worship Yahweh, and she worships according to the custom of the Druze as I have explained. Will your faith allow you to marry a woman who worships and sacrifices to another god?"

Moses shifted from one foot to another and looked at Zipporah as he answered Reuel, "No father. I cannot marry a pagan. The woman I marry must worship Yahweh and any children must be raised to worship Yahweh."

Zipporah nodded and said, "We Druze believe that when a man and a woman live together as man and wife, they must indeed be one. I am willing to confess Yahweh as the one true God. I will worship him; I will raise our children according to your wishes. I will accept your leadership not only as the head of our family, the leader of our new branch and as the priest of our Yahweh.

Reuel clapped his hands and said, "That is as it should be. Moses, I have one more question for you. My daughter is not just dark skinned, she has black skin. Her children will be black skinned. Will you love, honor, and protect her and her children the same as you would a white skinned woman and her children?"

Moses laughed, "Father, I can see that Zipporah is black. My affection for her goes beyond the color of her skin. I admit that her propensity to be strong willed might cause some conflict, but we will work through that. But back to the issue of children, you brought the subject up, so I just want to be sure that you know there will be children."

Reuel laughed again and said, "Moses, I am sending my daughter with you knowing what is going to happen when a woman and a man live together. Yes, and I am going to make a public declaration this morning blessing your union and the issue from that union."

Zipporah sighed and said, "Well let's get on with it, our people are gathering, the herdsmen have the flock out of the night enclosure, our pack animals are loaded, all is ready father. We wait only on you."

Reuel place his hand on Moses' shoulder and moved him gently in place beside Zipporah. He lifted his voice so all the crowd could hear and said, "In the sight of God and by the authority vested in me as the leader of this clan, I now proclaim, that I have given my daughter Zipporah as wife to this man Moses. It is lawful for them to co-habit as man and wife and I pray that their union may be fruitful. You are all witness to this my proclamation."

Reuel kissed Zipporah on the cheek, slapped Moses on the back and said, "Sunrise is over, and the day waits for no man. Go now, keep your watch and send me a messenger now and again with news of my grandchildren and how the new branch of our clan goes."

Moses took Zipporah by the hand and stepped in front of those assembled to go with them, "Joshua, take charge of the flock and add ten goats, Zipporah favors goat cheese."

He waited as Joshua collected the goats and added five new volunteers who stepped forward at the last minute with their families wanting to serve with him as herdsmen then he turned his back to the rising sun and led his new clan north by west into the desert. He glanced back once and Zipporah said, "Don't look back Moses, sunrise is over, you are out of Egypt, and we are now committed to the new day."

Chapter Nineteen

North To Horeb

Moses stood on the rocky outcropping and watched his son working the sheep down the mountainside to the valley below. He could hear the water cascading along the riverbed carved by centuries of snowmelt just like that watering this lush little valley now.

As he watched, he saw the lead sheep turn and run from the sound of the rushing water. Moses cupped his hands and shouted, "Turn her, Gershom, take her by the halter and lead her to the pond away from the rushing water."

He could tell that his son did not hear him but smiled when Gershom took the lamb by the halter and led her to the quiet water. The rest of the flock followed and were soon grazing on the lush spring growth or wading into the shallow pond for a long drink. *'The boy has the instinct of his grandfather,'* Moses thought.

Moses sat on the stone and watched his son move among the sheep. He nodded in approval as Gershom bent to check the eyes and ears of one then another. Moses thought, *I am a stranger here, doing that which I have no knack for, but Gershom is born to this. He is as adept at managing the sheep as was Joshua.* The thought of Joshua brought sadness to Moses. Joshua had been his right hand for thirty years. Moses sighed, remembering the morning Sarah had come crying to his tent with the news that she could not wake Joshua. Moses had run to the tent and found his friend cold to the touch. He had died early in the night, and his body was already stiffening.

That had been some ten years back, Sarah had lasted five years after Joshua, and now she was gone. Moses thought about those who had come with him into the Northwest desert of Midian. Most of them had died, and now their children populated the region given to Moses by Jethro.

Moses looked to the pond and saw Gershom waving for him to come. He strolled down the slope and said, "You did well son, you have your grandfathers' gift with these animals."

Gershom waved his hand over the flock and said, "Dad, we need to move this flock to Horeb."

"Horeb, son? That is the backside of our region."

“I know, dad, but we have seven hundred sheep in this little cove. They will strip the grass to the roots by the end of the day; it will take a year to recover. We will need this as a stopping place before winter sets in. Yes, we must move them now, take them up Horeb, the snow will have melted in the higher glens and vales by now, and there will be plenty of grass and little pools of water."

Moses knew his son was right. "The morning is half gone, if we leave now and set a hard pace, darkness will find us at the base of the mountain. We will be well-positioned to start the climb at first light tomorrow. Let's go now."

Gershom ran his shepherds' crook under the lead sheep's halter, turned it, and drew it back, so he was in total control of her. He stepped forward, bent, and attached two bells to the harness, one on each of her shoulders. Satisfied, he stood and pushed her forward. She stepped forward, and the bells rang out. The flock fell in line behind her. Moses waited until the last sheep passed and then stepped in behind to keep the rear guard. He used his staff to bring a couple of the lambs back into line and looked to Horeb.

The walk was long and uneventful. Moses trudged along behind the flock, and his mind began to wander, *'Forty years I have been following sheep in the Midian desert. While in Egypt, my people suffer under the heavy hand of Seti. Last week, the caravan brought news that Seti is dying, and that Ramses is preparing to take control as pharaoh. If memory serves me correctly, Egyptian law prevents a pharaoh from imposing a sentence for an offense that occurred before he became pharaoh. That means the death sentence imposed by Seti for my killing the Egyptian will die with him. I will be a free man once Ramses is the pharaoh.*

Free to do what? God, please tell me, am I destined to follow sheep all my life? Is all my education, all my training on how to lead people to be wasted?"

"Dad, dad!" Gershom's yelling pulled Moses out of his fog. Moses saw now that the sheep were beginning to scatter, then he saw the bear. Moses ran toward the bear, thinking, *'Why didn't I remember that the bears would be coming out of their winters' hibernation?'*

Moses realized this was a young bear, probably facing his first spring without his mother. The cub saw Moses and turned to face him. The cub stood erect, facing Moses. Moses shouted and ran to the bear, reaching for his sling and stones in his pouch but decided to use his rod instead. Moses moved his staff to his left hand and lifted his rod with his right hand. He struck the young bear on the tip of his snout. Blood flushed forth, and the youngster yelped in pain. He dropped to his all fours and trotted away from Moses. He stopped and looked back, clearly confused, and surprised that this man had charged him. Moses stepped toward him and yelled. That was all it took; the cub ran from his tormentor. Moses called to Gershom to continue toward Horeb at a faster pace. He followed along, keeping a watchful eye out for the awakening hungry bears.

Dusk found them at the base of Mount Horeb. Gershom led the bell sheep in an ever-tightening loop; finally, he had the flock in a compact pack circle and allowed the tired animals to lie down. Moses and Gershom gathered dried brush and set fires surrounding the herd. It seemed the sheep sensed the fires would keep predators at bay. Moses climbed atop a boulder on one side of the flock, and Gershom did the same on the opposite side. They both drew bread and cheese from their packs and settled in for the night.

The night passed quietly, and as the fourth watch began, Moses stepped down from the rock and kneeled in prayer. "Lord, lead me, show me you will today. Make it clear, and I will do that which you require."

As he stood to face the rising sun, Moses felt the need to kneel again and consider the thoughts running through his mind, "*I am now eighty years old. My first forty years were spent in the pharaoh's court, as a prince of Egypt. I am educated as an Egyptian.*

I have been a fugitive from Pharaoh: A stranger in a foreign land the last forty years. In Egypt, people followed me because I commanded them; here, I have learned how to convince people to follow me, I know how to help people survive in the wilderness, the importance of unity, and focusing on purpose. I can feel a change coming, and I wonder if I am ready for it.

Moses stood and called to his son, "Gershom, let's move them up the slope; I want to be in the first vale by mid-day. We have pushed them hard; today, we will allow them to feed, take water, and rest the second half of the day."

Gershom led the bell sheep up the slope, and the flock fell in line behind her. Moses waited until the last of the flock was out of the night camp and followed.

Noon found them in a small hollow halfway up the mountain. The snowmelt had not dried up and was collected in a small crevice at the hollow's bottom. The slopes on either side were filled with tender spring grasses. Higher up, where the sun was able to shine on the hill all day, the spring growth had already dried.

Gershom sat at the opening of the hollow and unrolled his cheese and bread. Moses climbed above the flock so he could see the approaches on both sides of the grazing flock.

Moses looked down to where Gershom sat watching over the flock. He felt that familiar rush of love for his son, his firstborn. *'How I love that boy, there is nothing I will not do for him.'*

A warm breeze swept across the mountain, and Moses heard a soft voice borne by the breeze, *'Moses, I am your God, I love you as I love your son.'*

Moses looked to the peak from whence it came; he was overcome with the beauty, the colorful spring flowers of the lower slope highlighted against the brightness of the yet to melt snowfields on the peaks.

Moses stood and whistled. When Gershom looked his way, he pointed up the slope. Gershom waved his understanding, and Moses walked toward the peak.

Halfway to the top, Moses smelled smoke; then he saw a plume wafting up from a crevice; he walked toward the smoke and saw a flame sprouting from the middle of a large bush. It struck Moses that the flame was coming from the midst of the bush, yet the bush's outer limbs were not on fire, and none of the bush was being consumed by the fire. Moses was amazed and turned aside to take a closer look.

He stepped down into the crevice and approached the bush. As he approached the bush, Moses heard his name called, 'Moses, Moses.'

He answered, 'Here I am."

The same voice that had called his name said, "Do not draw near this place. Take your sandals off your feet, for the place where you stand is holy ground. I am the God of Abraham, the God of Isaac, and the God of Jacob.

A great fear passed over Moses, and he covered his face with his hands, for he was afraid to look upon God. Moses dropped to his knees, stretched full length on the ground in front of the bush; his heart was pounding, and the pulse drummed in his ears.

He lay prostrate before his Lord for the next hour: He knew that the voice coming from the bush was the voice of his God. He heard the voice say that He, had heard the cries of the Hebrews in Egypt and that the voice in bush represented his coming down to deliver the Hebrews from captivity. Moses realized that the bush represented Israel and that the flame in the midst of the bush, represented Gods' wish to be in the heart of his people. He was given to know that the foliage not burning, and the bush not being consumed illustrated the sovereign power God held over the natural laws of His creation.

He also knew that he was to return to Egypt, confront the pharaoh, and lead the Hebrews into the wilderness where they were to worship God. He had a vague understanding that their deliverance would be through the wilderness and that if it remained a place of worship, the journey would go well. At the end of that journey, they would enter a land that God had promised Abraham they would own. Moses knew they would be delivered from want into plenty.

Chapter Twenty

The Return

Moses lay still waiting for the voice to speak again. When the silence grew deep, he lifted his face from the dirt and looked at the bush. The fire burned no more, and the voice spoke no more. But Moses still had questions; *Why him? Who was he to confront the pharaoh? Why would the Hebrews trust him to lead them? What would he say if they asked by whose authority he came?*

These thoughts rushed from his mind into his heart. Moses was fearful. As he examined each question, he felt rather than heard the answer. Moses came to understand that God was not showing him the totality of what was to be. He was showing Moses what he could handle, a small portion. Finally, Moses stood and moved away from the bush. After a few steps, he glanced over his shoulder; there stood the bush, no flame, no indication there had been a flame in its' midst. Just the bush, standing tall and deeply rooted on the mountainside. Moses smiled and turned into his destiny.

Moses made his way down the mountain and returned to Jethro's camp. He entered the tent and said to his father-in-law, "Please, let me return to Egypt, to my brethren to see if they are still alive."

Jethro nodded and said, "Go in peace."

As Moses gathered his family in preparation for the trip, he heard the Lord say, "*Go, return to Egypt without fear; for all the men who sought your life are dead.*"

Moses nodded his understanding and led his family out of Jethro's camp. He turned southeast toward Egypt. On the third day of his journey, Moses saw the palm trees of the oasis where he spent the first night of his run from pharaoh. He led his family into the cool depression, watered his stock, then knelt before the pool to wash his face.

Moses looked at his reflection; he remembered looking at the reflection of his young face forty years before. So much had changed; Seti was Pharoah and had issued the death warrant after Moses killed the Egyptian. Now he studied this image before him; the past forty years had changed him, he doubted that Seti would recognize him, but that was now a moot point because the Lord had said that all the men who sought him were now dead. According to Egyptian law, the death warrant dies with the pharaoh who issued it. If Seti was dead, Ramses II would be pharaoh, but Ramses was barred from issuing a death warrant for an offense that occurred before he became pharaoh. As Moses studied his reflection, he heard the voice of God," *When you go back to Egypt, I will have you confront Ramses. When the time is right, I will enable you to perform miracles before him. I command you to be obedient and do all those, wonders before pharaoh, that I put in your hand,*"

Moses thought, will these wonders so impress Ramses that he will let the Hebrews go? God answered instantly, "*I will harden his heart, and he will not let the people go. You are to say to him, 'Israel is my son, my firstborn. Let my son go that he may serve me. If you refuse, I will kill your firstborn.'*"

Moses shook his head thinking, threatening the pharaoh or his family is a capital offense. '*Even if he does not seek to kill me, he will not be able to relent because his court will see it as a sign of weakness, proof that he fears the word of God. He will be in a box. He cannot let the people go. Is this the plan of God?'*

As Moses thought through this, he noticed that his reflection faded, the water became cloudy, and his ability to reason and understand the thoughts rushing through his mind vanished. Moses became dizzy, his vision blurred, and he felt a weight pressing against his chest; a sharp pain followed the pressure. He struggled for breath. Moses fell onto his right side. He was immobilized; fear grasped him as he realized that he was dying. "Why Lord," he gasped. He heard no answer. Moses pushed himself onto his knees and then forced his legs to lift him to his feet.

He heard the voice of his wife, Zipporah, calling his name, "Moses, look at me my husband of blood." He turned to see her approaching; she was holding a bloody stone in her left hand and a piece of bloody flesh in her right; she cast the flesh at his feet and said, "He is circumcised."

"What are you talking about?" Moses was stunned.

"God appeared to me in a dream last night and told me that he was angry with you because saw you followed my tradition and did not circumcise our son as his covenant with Abraham required. The Lord told me that we are one, you and I, so the sin rests on us both. He understands our frailties, but He demands obedience from those He plans to use. I knew that His plans for you would not go forward until we both came into obedience. I saw you collapse and knew that we could not go forward until we came into obedience.

So, I took a sharp stone and circumcised our son. There at your feet is the restoration of the blood covenant between you and God. We are now clean and ready to be used for His purpose, my husband of blood. One last thing God told me, *'There are two major weakness in our union; You tend to think that you can deviate from that which he tells you to do. He told me, my will is to be done here on earth as sure as it is in heaven. And we both have intemperate passions. We must temper our passions to his will."*

Moses watched Zipporah as she walked away. A voice surfaced from the deep recesses of his memory; he heard Ramses II saying, "*if your past is any indicator of your future, you hear but do not follow instructions. You tend to act as you think best, which, I prophesy, will prove to be the very thing that will keep you from fulfilling your destiny. I predict Moses that your inattention to detail will cause you to be left behind while others step into the fulness of their promise."*

Moses moved into the shade of a palm and sat with his back resting against the rough bark. A cool breeze swept through the shaded glen, and Moses fell asleep. In his sleep, Moses found himself standing before the burning bush again. He bowed before the flame and asked, "Why Lord? You knew I had broken covenant when you chose me; you knew when you gave me instruction. So why wait until this encampment to strike me?" The flame glowed brightly, and Moses heard, " *'You stood before witnesses and told Jethro that you would lead your wife and your house to be obedient to my commandments and that you would worship me, not the gods of the Druze. Yet, you failed to lead and allowed your wife to break covenant with me by refusing to circumcise your son. You both knew what to do and did it not, to you that was a sin. I spoke to Zipporah in a dream and told her that she led you astray and that she needed to come into obedience so that you and I could walk in covenant again. You are restored, I can use you, and I have the next part of the plan in motion. Rest in my sovereignty, trust in my sufficiency. Remember what I said? I Am What I Am. Moses, that means that I will be there when I need to be there with what is required to complete my plan.'*

Moses woke with peace in his heart.

Moses walked to the stream, kneeled, and looked into water. The cloudiness was gone, the water was clear, and Moses saw his reflection as it was forty years before, when Gershom was born. '*God has restored me.*' Was his thought.

Moses stood, called for Zipporah and told her, "We are seven days travel from the Egyptian border. God has called me to go to Mount Sinai tomorrow morning. My brother Aaron will meet me there. You will remain encamped here until we return. We will have the word of the Lord and put His plan into action."

Chapter Twenty-One

The Meeting on Mount Sinai

Aaron was awakened by the early morning chill seeping through his blankets. He sat up, stretched, and wiped the sleep out of his eyes. His legs were cramping, and he pushed them out in front of him; as he did, some loose stones were dislodged. He watched them roll forward and disappear. He heard them striking other rocks and then the sound of the stones striking water somewhere in the deep darkness beyond his feet.

Aaron reached over his shoulders and felt the limestone's hard rough surface against which he had slept. He stood carefully, using the stone as both a brace and anchor. He sidestepped along the shelf until he found the notch in the rock through which he had slid down through the night onto the shelf hours before. He climbed up the natural steps and sat down. The sun was now peeking over the Mountain opposite where he sat, and he could see that he had slept on the edge of a natural outcropping of stone along a canyon wall. He shook his head in wonder as he peered over the edge at the drop that he would have experienced had he rolled over in the middle of the night.

Now he stood and looked across the narrow slot in the earth to the Sinai on the other side. He gathered his robe, wrapping it around his legs to ward off the sharp breeze, and stepped out along the top of the drop, looking for the way down and across the stream that the shepherds had told him was the way into the wilderness. Finding the trail, he descended, waded across the trickle of water and into the Sinai. Ahead he could see Mt. Sinai. The snow-capped peak shined brightly in the morning sun. Aaron walked on in obedience to the compulsion he had to climb Sinai. He knew that God had sent him but for what purpose.

He trudged through the morning and found himself at the base of the great mountain as the noon sun baked the wilderness.

Turning, he glanced back along the route that had brought him to this point and was surprised to see a man walking toward him. The man was leading a mule. Aaron gasped as he recognized the movement of the man; it was Moses, his baby brother. Aaron ran to Moses, embraced, and kissed his brother on the cheek.

Chapter Twenty-Two

Moses and Aaron Meet on God's Mountain

Moses and Aaron wrapped their arms around each other and danced in a circle, rejoicing, and giving thanks to God for bringing them together. They danced until they were out of breath. Then they collapsed in the shade of a giant boulder but continued to hold each other. They laughed and talked into the night, erasing the forty years that had separated them, they were together again, and each sensed that God had ordained this time, this reunion for some special purpose.

"Moses, what is this? Why has God brought us together here on His mountain after forty years of separation?"

Moses told Aaron about the flame in the midst of the bush; he repeated each instruction God had given him. He told Aaron, "I cannot speak clearly. I still have the speech impediment; I still struggle to put a sentence together coherently. But you, you, my brother, are as eloquent as ever. You speak with confidence; your voice is strong, and authority flows from your tongue. You will be by my side; you will be my voice when I need you."

Aaron saw that there would be times when his brother would need him, and his spirit witnessed the call of God on the two of them to work as one to deliver the people from Pharaoh.

"How do we start, Moses?"

"We start by gathering the Elders of Israel, explaining God's plan, seeking their approval, and ask them to agree with us in prayer. Finally, we lead them in worshiping our Lord, and then my brother, we go to the Pharaoh, asking him to free the people. We go in the name of the Great I Am.

The brothers kneeled in prayer; they rose, ate a supper of bread and cheese, wrapped up in their blankets and slept. The morning found them refreshed and eager to step into their destiny. They moved out to gather the Elders.

Chapter Twenty-Three

The Sheep Market

"Aaron, I have been gone forty years; none of those who lead our people know me. They know and respect you. You take the lead, introduce me and help me to encourage them to meet with us in the wilderness at the foot of Gods' Mountain."

"I will, Moses, but you must stand beside me. They may not know you, but they know of you. Their grandfathers and fathers have told them of the Hebrew who was raised a Prince of Egypt but rejected a royal's life to honor his lineage and killed an Egyptian while protecting his Hebrew brothers.

You are a legend, but many fault you for not staying. It is a common opinion that with your military training and experience, you could have led our people in a revolt against the Pharaoh. A great many believe that we could have had our freedom forty years ago. There will be those who ask why you have waited all these years to lead us out of captivity. You must be ready to answer."

"I see. Tell me. Who do the Elders look to as their leader?"

"They look to a man named Cyrus. He claims to be a direct descendant of Abraham. He is the key to winning the support of the Elders."

"Good, let's go to him first."

"Yes, he will expect you to call on him, to pay your respects, and to come bearing a gift worthy of his position. He has the largest flock of sheep among our people. He prides himself on being the best breeder among us. A prize ram would be appropriate.

Moses, while it is essential to honor Cyrus, I think you should consider moving among the people, let them hear you assert your lineage as a Hebrew, tell them of the last forty years as a shepherd on the backside of the desert. Don't assume leadership; let them elevate you, and they will. One thing you will have to address is why you married a Cushite woman. You should consider sending her back to her father, at least for now."

"There are a lot of things to consider. I will not apologize for my marriage to Zipporah; she has been a good wife. To my way of thinking, it is a non-subject. Secondly, I will tell them how I took a group of people and led them to a new region and established a community where the God of our father Abraham is worshiped, and the Hebrews' traditions are observed. I am anxious to establish a relationship within our community, to live as a Hebrew. As for the ram, I left my flock with my father-in-law. Where will I get a ram?"

"The ram should be from our local flock, and we will speak of it being a gift to honor Cyrus. He will hear of it before we meet and will be pleased that you are honoring him before the people."

Moses followed his brother Aaron into the sheep market. It was well past mid-day, and the Egyptian heat was bouncing off the ground in shimmering waves. The odor of the animals pushed together in such a confined space was magnified by the heat. Aaron pointed to a tall, thin man and said to Moses, "His name is Effrin. He has the best sheep in the market, and he knows it. His price will be high, but a ram from his flock will be a prized gift. Come, let me introduce you. Be prepared; he has a sharp tongue and a caustic personality. He is well known for his opinion that you are more legend than fact."

Moses nodded and stepped in front of Aaron, "Greetings, Effrin. I am Moses, who you have declared to be more legend than fact. Come, touch me, feel my flesh, test my bones and see that the legend lives."

Moses' voice had carried to the people around Effrins' stall, and they rushed forward to get a look at this gaunt figure claiming to be the legend they had grown up hearing about. They pressed in, touching Moses.

Effrin stepped forward, waving the people out of his way. "Moses, you say. If you are him, tell us why you return, what you expect to find hereafter forty years' absence, and tell us if you are returning as a Prince of Egypt or as a Hebrew."

"Fair enough, Effrin. I am indeed a Prince of Egypt by the decree of Pharaoh, but I was born a Hebrew, a son of Abraham, descended from the tribe of Levi. I return as a Hebrew expecting to find my place among my people; I come, sent by God to meet with Cyrus and the Elders to plan our Exodus from Egypt and captivity."

"Careful Moses, you are speaking treason, and the Pharoah has ears everywhere, even here among us. But since you have broached the subject, where would this Exodus lead, where would we find freedom?"

"Let those who inform Pharaoh hurry to him with this message, our people will be free, either he lets us go, or our God will deal harshly with him. Our freedom lies beyond Egypt in a land our Lord has reserved for us. But for today I have come to buy a gift for Cyrus. I wish to honor him as the leader of our Elders. I know he is renowned as a breeder, and I seek your very best ram as a gift for him. Come, show me your best and let us close the deal."

The talk of freedom, of an Exodus to land reserved for the Hebrews set the crowd to buzzing; the people pressed in around Moses and Aaron, shouting questions and asking if he or Cyrus would lead their Exodus.

Moses held up his hand and pleaded, "Please let me buy the ram and go to Cyrus. Listen for news from your Elder. We will move quickly on this. Your freedom is at hand. You should start preparing by gathering your valuables; we will not leave Egypt empty-handed. Rest your animals, feed them well, keep them hydrated, set food aside and be ready to move at any time night or day."

Effrin led Moses to his prize ram and said, "you say this ram is a gift to Cyrus to honor his leadership, and I take it to persuade him to go along with your plan, to speak to the people, and to encourage them to follow you. What assurance do you offer me what you say is true?"

Moses started to speak but began to stutter. Aaron spoke up, "You don't know my brother Effrin, but you know me. I give you my word that all Moses has said is true."

Effrin nodded slowly and said, "That is good enough for me. I want to be a part of this historic event. Take the ram as my contribution and let history record that I was the first of the Hebrews to enlist in the Exodus."

Moses clapped Effrin on the shoulder and said, "It will be as you say; I will tell Cyrus of your generosity and record it in the history of the Exodus."

He took the rope and led the ram away from the market.

Chapter Twenty-Four

The Sheep Gate

The crowd followed along, calling questions to Moses and Aaron, "When will you meet with the Elders? When will we know the plan? How will we stand against Pharoah and the Army? How will you protect us?"

Aaron said to Moses, "Brother, you may have spoken too soon and too boldly. As Effrin said, Pharaoh has ears everywhere. You can be sure he has heard of your declaration already. I suggest we not wait; let's go to Cyrus now before we are arrested and taken to Pharaoh."

"I agree; where will we find Cyrus this time of day?"

"This is the time of day that the flocks to are brought inside the walls for the night. The pens and water troughs are inside the sheep gate. That is where we will find Cyrus."

"Lead the way, brother, or do I just follow my nose?"

Aaron laughed and said, "The smell gets stronger as the flocks enter but turn to your right at the next street, and we will walk directly to the sheep gate."

Moses tugged the reluctant ram into the turn and saw a giant of a man striding toward him. He had a leathery face, chiseled by years in the desert sun and wind. He launched a rousing laugh across the space between them as this giant reached his hand toward Moses and said, "Ho Moses, you do not remember me, of course, but I was one of those '*villagers*' rescued by you and the defenders, during your military training long ago, I bid you welcome home. The news of your return and your mission runs through the streets. I see the ram is as magnificent as I was told. Come, sit and let me hear how I can help with your mission."

Moses and Aaron followed Cyrus to a couple of benches inside the sheep gate. Cyrus pulled the benches together, so they faced each other. Moses and Aaron sat next to each other on one bench, and Cyrus sat alone on the opposite bench facing them.

____

Elder Cyrus, thank you for receiving me. I come; sent by the God of our father, Abraham. He spoke to me from a flame in a bush on the backside of the Midian desert. He told me that he had heard the suffering of our people and that he had come down in the form of the flame to tell me that He was going to use me to lead our people out of Egypt, out of bondage and into a land that He had chosen for us, just us. He is going to establish us as a people, as a nation. I come to you, the chief Elder seeking your support. I first want to gather the Elders together in the wilderness at the foot of God's Mountain. I will tell them all that God has spoken; then, we will pray and worship.

____

The crowd had pressed around Moses and Cyrus, but now they withdrew and parted creating a clear passage leading to the benches where the two sat talking. Alerted by the sudden silence, Moses and Cyrus saw a contingent of soldiers approaching. Moses saw that he was the focus of the officer leading the troops.

The officer asked, "Are you, Moses?"

"I am Moses; who are you?"

"I am Razi, Captain of the palace guard. The Pharoah has sent me to escort you to his court."

"So, you are Captain of the Palace guard, which means you are an active-duty member of the Egyptian army, correct?"

"Yes."

"Tell me, Captain. Why do you not respect me as a member of the royal family and an officer in the Egyptian Army?

Moses saw Razi stiffen as he realized the seriousness of his error. He dropped to one knee and bowed from the waist. "Please forgive me, Highness. I meant no disrespect. Ramses requests your presence, and I am honored to provide you safe passage to his court."

Moses nodded and said, "Stand, Captain. You are forgiven; I left Egypt before you were born, and you cannot be expected to know my history. Would you please convey my respect to Pharoah and tell him that I must meet with the Elders of the Hebrews? I will come to his court as soon as I conclude my business with them. You are dismissed, Captain."

"But Highness, Pharoah will be angry when I return without you."

"Captain, you tell him that I invoked my privilege as a member of the royal family and dismissed you. He would be angrier should you fail to respect that."

The captain nodded, saluted Moses, and asked, "May I withdraw highness?"

"You may."

Cyrus sighed and said, "You bait the bear, Moses. Come, let us gather the Elders and meet before Ramses sends more soldiers."

Moses knew Cyrus was right and rose to follow the Elder as he left to gather the Elders.

Chapter Twenty-Five

The Elders

Aaron and Moses followed Cyrus to the town square. The crowd trailed along behind. Cyrus sat on the edge of the fountain, dipped his hand in the cool water, and ran it through his thinning hair. Refreshed, he motioned two of the men in the crowd to approach. "Go, tell the Elders to meet me at the foot of Gods' mountain tomorrow at sunrise. Tell Eli to take charge and have the Elders assembled as the sun casts its' first rays over the peak of the Mountain."

The men left the square hurrying to obey Cyrus. "They will ensure the message is delivered. You both need to get a good nights' rest; you must be ready to lead worship and then to answer the many questions the Elders will have."

Moses nodded and said, "We will sleep in the brush at the foot of the mountain; sunrise will find us there and ready."

He stood and led Aaron to the stream and then into the brush. Finding a spot free of stones, they made a pile of dry wood and started a small fire; sitting by the fire, they ate the last of their bread and cheese, wrapped their robes tightly against the chill of the night, and lay down to sleep.

Moses tossed and turned, unable to find sleep. *'I told Cyrus that the dawn would find me ready to answer the questions the Elders will have, but will I be ready?*

Here I am, an eighty-year-old man who they do not know, and I am going to stand before them and tell them that God appeared to me as a flame in a bush that the flame could not consume. And that He is sending me to lead them in demanding liberation from the most powerful man in the world. They will think me a mad man. And I am supposed to quell their doubts with a couple of magic tricks. They will never risk their lives; all that they have to follow me.' he mused.

Finally, he rolled to his knees and bowed his head, "Lord, You have revealed Yourself and your will to me. I come in obedience but confess that I fear the Elders will not find me worthy of leading. My heart is full of desire to accomplish all you have called me to; I trust you to cause my tongue to reveal the fullness of my heart. Now, I pray that you will give me peace and allow me to rest."

Moses finished his prayer and lay down again. He placed his hand under his head as a cushion. As he drifted into sleep, he heard the voice from the bush say, "*So be it.*" Peace flooded him, and Moses slept.

Aaron shook Moses awake and said, "It is time to get up brother, the first group is crossing the stream now."

Moses sat, rubbed the sleep from his eyes, and cupped his hands to receive the cold-water Aaron offered. He splashed the water on his face and stood to welcome the first arrivals.

"Good morning, elders. Thank you for coming; sit here and start to form a semi-circle, so those coming after will see how we want to be arrayed."

Moses left Aaron to greet the elders as they arrived and stepped behind a grouping of large stones to pray. Moses kneeled, lifted his hand to the heavens, and said, "I go before these elders in your name. Do not leave me, lead and I will follow."

He rose from prayer and faced the elders. He heard the voice from the burning bush again, *'Lead them in worship. I want to hear them declare that there is no God but me. I want them to declare that they will follow and obey me. I want them to acknowledge me as the God of their father, Abraham. I want them to express their belief that I Am what they need when they need it.*

Then tell them what you witnessed at the bush, repeat all that I told you. They must confess that they believe, unbelief will keep them in bondage. Tell them that I sent you to deliver them from Pharaoh's hand and that I have prepared land that they and their sons will own forever. Tell them that you will lead them in the Exodus from slavery into freedom but that none may take part in the journey who do not believe or who will not declare my Lordship. Tell them that none who have failed to honor the blood covenant between Abraham and me, may go. Neither father nor uncircumcised son."

Cyrus stood before the elders to introduce Moses, "Elders, most of you have never met Moses, but you have all heard his story. He was born a Hebrew. His parents hid him to thwart Pharaoh's order that all our newborn sons should be killed, pulled from the Nile by Queen Hatsheput, raised in the palace, declared a prince of Egypt by Seti, a beneficiary of the training and education given all children of the ruling class, killed an Egyptian in defense of a Hebrew and had to flee to Midian where he has spent the last forty years of his life. In the backside of the desert, the Lord our God appeared to him as a flame in a bush that was not consumed, with a message for us. I have heard his message and believe God sends him. He is here now to deliver the message to you."

Cyrus stepped aside, and Moses stood in front of the elders. He nodded his appreciation to Cyrus and launched into his message. The words flowed from him like water loosed from a broken dam. After two hours, he stopped and scanned the faces before him. On some, he saw doubt; on some, he saw acceptance, but on all, he saw hope that their bondage was at an end and a willingness to follow that hope.

Moses let the silence grow deeper, and a young man, Moses guessed him to be the youngest of the elders, spoke, "Pardon me Moses, my name is Zev, and I am young to be questioning one of your age and stature, but I have to ask, *'Do you expect us to risk losing all we have by following an eighty-year-old man as he confronts Pharaoh demanding that he let us go? Are we to believe that God spoke to you from a burning bush on the backside of the Midian desert? I say no, I will have to have something besides such a fanciful tale before risking all to follow you.*

Moses nodded and replied, "Well said, Zev, and I told God that there would be those who doubted my sanity and His call. He told me to perform these wonders to convince you that He sent me. Watch Zev." Moses cast his staff on the ground in front of Zev, and it turned into a serpent. Zev gasped and tried to escape. Moses said, "Stay where you are, Zev and watch. Moses then grabbed the serpent by the tail. It became his staff once more. He handed the staff to Zev and said, examine it; is it not a common staff?"

Zev hesitated but took the staff. He pounded it against the ground, ran his hands over it, and said, "A magician's trick with his staff is supposed to convince me?"

Moses chuckled and said, "Trick with my staff? Okay, you cast it on the ground."

Zev hurled the staff onto the ground and watched as it lay inert in the dirt. Moses could see on the young mans' face that he was not convinced.

He extended his hand to Zev and said, "Look at the hand, do you see any sign of disease, or does it appear clean?" Zev took Moses' hand, turned it over, and examined it carefully. The hand is normal and healthy; why do you ask this?"

Moses thrust his hand into his robe and withdrew it quickly. He extended it to Zev and said, "And now?"

Zev stepped away from the extended hand, for it was now "covered in leprosy."

Moses said, now watch God prove himself, "He thrust the hand into his robe and withdrew it once more. The hand was clean and healthy."

Moses could see that Zev was still doubtful; he turned to Aaron and said, "bring me a cup of water from the stream." All the men turned to watch Aaron dip the cup into the spring and bring the water to Moses. Moses handed it to Zev and said, "Examine it closely, dip your finger into it, taste it if you like, and then tell your brothers what it is."

Zev dipped his finger in the water and raised that finger to his mouth; he licked his finger and said, "It is water, a little musty smelling but water nevertheless."

Moses said, "hand the cup to me."

Zev did as requested and watched as Moses poured the water onto the ground. The water pooled in the desert sand and then turned red.

Zev fell to his knees and looked closely at the red liquid. He dipped his finger in the blood and held it up for the others to see. "It is blood; he turned the water from the stream into blood."

Moses said, "It is no magic trick; it is what God told me to do should you doubt me. I am his messenger; he is the I AM; he controls the natural and supernatural. I am asking that you follow God, not me, as He uses me to guide you to your inheritance."

He answered questions for another hour and then said, "In answer to the most asked question, *'when do we start?'* I say this; we have started by coming together here at the foot of Gods' Mountain. Tomorrow we go to Pharaoh and ask him to let us go on a three-day journey into the wilderness to sacrifice and worship God. He will refuse, and by doing so, he sets God's plan in motion."

Tomorrow morning, we will confront the most powerful natural an on earth and demand our freedom in compliance with the word of our supernatural God.

Chapter Twenty-Six

THE SUPERNATURAL CONFRONTS THE NATURAL

Moses stood on the captains' deck of the barge. A soft west wind was pushing the barge toward the bank. Moses pointed to a spot where the bank extended out into the Nile. "Immediately past that point is a small cove. The basket my mother put me adrift in floated into that cove. There is where I was drawn from the Nile. Put us ashore there."

The pilot directed the barge toward the point. The wind caught the aft beam and rushed the barge forward; Moses could see that the landing would be rough. "Brace yourself," he called to the elders seated on benches amidship.

The palace was now visible from the elevated deck on which he stood. Moses shaded his eyes from the sun hanging low in the morning's eastern sky. The barge nosed into the little beach, and Moses led his party ashore. Without looking back, he climbed the slope and stood examining the entrance to the palace. Two members of the palace guard stood at the bottom of the steps leading up to the terrace.

One moved in front of the steps and held his hand up to stop Moses from entering the palace. Moses and the elders stopped, and the young Egyptian asked, "Who are you, and why do you seek to enter the palace through the royal family entrance?"

"I am Moses, a Prince of Egypt by order of Seti when he was Pharaoh. I am accustomed to using this entrance. I am here at the command of Ramses." Moses responded.

The officer bowed and said, "Good morning, Highness. We were told to expect you. I will escort you to Pharaoh's court."

"That is not necessary; I know the way.

"Yes, Highness, but my presence will ensure you are not bothered by other members of the guard, and I will count it an honor to announce you. Are all of these Hebrews going into the court with you?"

"Yes. Lead the way, please."

Moses followed the officer up the steps and onto the landing. He paused, looked back at the Nile, and remembered that this is the very spot from which he fled Egypt forty years before.

"Wait here, highness; as I announce you, how should I announce those who accompany you?"

"Announce them as the elders of Israel."

The officer nodded and pulled the bell cord to prepare the court that visitors were about to be announced, "The buzz of voices from inside the chamber stopped as the members anticipated the entrance of visitors.

"Most honorable pharaoh now comes His Highness, Prince Moses; accompanied by the elders of Israel," the officer announced.

Moses stepped through the entrance, bowed, and said, "Good morning, pharaoh, I am here in obedience to your command."

"I commanded your presence, Moses, not the elders of Israel."

"Yes, majesty, but we have come to you representing the Hebrew people who from this day forward seek your recognition of us as the nation of Israel.

"You come as a nation, do you? Does that mean you are in rebellion against my realm?"

"No, Highness, we do not come as rebels. We come as captive people bearing a message from our God to you, our captor.

"So, the God of the Hebrews gives you a message for me; does he recognize me as your Pharaoh, Moses?"

"He does recognize you as Pharaoh, and it is to you in your official position as the ruler, the sovereign of Egypt, and the one who holds His people captive that He sends this message. *'Let my people go three days into the wilderness, thus out of your sight and immediate control, so that they may celebrate and worship me."*

Ramses gasped and sat back in his chair, "Let His people go? If I am their captive, then how is it that they are His people?"

"Pharaoh, we, the Hebrew people, practice Monotheism, we always have. We are descendants of Abraham, with who God made a covenant, that we would be a blessed people, masters of our fate, and owning all the land where we trod."

"We wish to go into the wilderness to confess of our acceptance of Him as the one true God, to pledge our obedience to follow Him and his ordinances, and to give thanks to Him who we worship; for increasing and prospering us, even while we are in captivity."

"Who is this God that I should head his voice? "Who is the Lord, that I should obey His voice to let Israel go? I do not know this Lord, nor will I let Israel go."

He sends you, a fugitive with blood on his hands; into my court with this request. Does He not hold you accountable for the Egyptian life you took?"

"I should not have killed the Egyptian, but I did so to prevent him from killing one of my own, a Hebrew."

"One of your own? Are you declaring yourself to be a Hebrew and not an Egyptian? Are you resigning your place in the Egyptian royal family and declaring your lot with the Hebrews come what may?

"Not at all; I cannot abandon a proclamation of a pharaoh, even a dead one, any more than you can nullify it. Seti said I am a prince of Egypt, I am and will be for as long as I live, but I was born a son of Abraham. I come here a prince; to answer a kings' command, but I also come as Abrahams' son and heir to the covenant between God and Abraham. I can no more cancel that than I can Seti's decree.

Since I came in obedience to your command, I claim the right of safe passage and protection from Pharaohs' anger that the rules of the royal court guarantee; for me and these with me. I call as witnesses the members of the court, who know that I come in response to a royal command.

"You shall have your safe passage this time. But your request for permission to lead my people into the wilderness and away from my supervision is denied."

"Moses stroked his beard and said, "Before you make your final decision, pharaoh, let me explain the circumstances of my coming here today."

Moses told Ramses about his encounter with the living God through the burning bush for the next forty-five minutes.

The chamber was silent; no one moved, not a word was heard. Moses finished and stepped back from the dais where Ramses sat staring at him.

"How dare you to come in here and insult my intelligence with such a tale! You expect us to believe that your invisible God manifested himself as a fire in the midst of a bush, and in all the time you were before him, the fire did not consume the fuel which fed it? Even if I chose to believe the rest of your story, how do you explain that contradiction of the laws of nature?"

"That is simple, Ramses. The fact that God chose to manifest Himself spectacularly does not diminish his supernatural being.

If you spend all your time focused on the spectacular in the supernatural; you will miss God.

In the natural, fire consumes that which feeds it, and in this instance, the fact that it did not is spectacular. But listen, Ramses; God lives outside of time, so it does not matter how long He was in the bush; nor was the bush feeding the fire, it was the supernatural presence of God that produced, the flame."

"Rubbish Moses. You spin your tale someplace else; I do not believe you."

"God told me that your heart would be hard and that you would not believe me. Therefore, he prepared me, a natural man, to perform three supernatural feats as evidence that this story I have told you is true."

"Really? I cannot wait to see this. Will you perform these supernatural feats as a prince of Egypt or as a son of Abraham?"

"I perform them as a servant of Yahweh."

Moses cast his staff at the feet of Ramses, and it turned into a serpent. Ramses gasped and moved away, his movement attracted the snake's attention, and it raised its' head and spread its hood, focusing on Ramses. Sit still, Pharaoh, and watch. Moses bent, took the serpent by the tail, and it turned into his staff. He leaned the staff toward Ramses and said, "Test it and see that the serpent focused on you a minute ago is nothing more than my staff."

Ramses declined the offer to handle the staff and said, "A cheap magician's trick, nothing more."

Moses nodded and extended his hand to Ramses, "Examine my hand, Pharaoh. Is it not clean and free of disease?"

"It is, so what?

Moses withdrew his hand, placed it inside his robe, and withdrew it again. The hand and wrist were covered in leprosy. Moses extended the hand again to Ramses. "Look at it now, pharaoh."

"Don't touch me, Moses."

Moses said, "Watch closely." He returned the hand inside the robe and withdrew it immediately. The hand was clean and free of the disease once more. "You see Pharaoh. Our God can bring affliction, and He can heal."

"Is that all Moses? This is proof of the existence of a supernatural God? I have magicians in my court who can do more spectacular things."

"You forget what I told you, Ramses. Focus on the spectacular in the supernatural, and you will miss God. The first two were designed to show you the power of our God. This last one is a precursor, an example of what to expect if you choose to ignore Him."

Moses reached into his pocket and removed a small cup. He dipped it in the water fountain and filled it with water. He held the cup for Ramses to inspect and said, "Water pharaoh. Water that brings and sustains life. But when touched by the wrath of God." Moses turned the cup up and poured the water from it; it turned to blood as the water fell to the floor. Moses continued to pour until the blood pooled in front of Ramses' throne. "Beware, Pharaoh, that you do not cause the wrath of our God to be poured out on this Kingdom.

God considers Israel his son. If you refuse his command to let his son, go; he will bring great affliction on your sons and this land. You will see the firstborn of Egypt die; you will see plagues, you will see pestilence, you will see drought, you will see famine."

"Do you threaten me, Moses?"

"No Ramses, I promise you will see these things come to pass if you refuse to let us go. And your refusal will not matter; because the covenant God made with our father Abraham supersedes any orders you may give to continue our captivity. In the end, we will go free."

Moses could see that Ramses was struggling to maintain his composure. "We will take our leave now, Highness. Do you agree that we can go three days into the wilderness and worship our God?"

"No, I do not. I accept the challenge of your God; let him manifest his supernatural powers. I will rule my people, including my servants, the Hebrews, through the manifest natural powers conferred on me as Pharaoh. Let' see who prevails as the master of Egypt and the Hebrews who would be known as Israel."

Moses bowed and backed out of the chamber. Once outside, he hurried the elders from the palace. As they boarded and pushed away from the bank into the middle of the Nile, Cyrus asked, "What next?"

Moses replied, "We were obedient to carry Gods' command to Pharaoh, but there will be repercussions. Not only will he double the watch on us to ensure we do not try to escape him, but we can expect him to punish us by increasing our workload and making our task harder.

Zev stood and said, "Forgive me, Moses and Cyrus, I know I am the youngest here, but if you will allow, I would like to summarize my understanding of what just happened."

Cyrus was irritated at Zevs' interruption, but Moses said, "Go ahead, Zev, let us hear from your perspective."

Zev stepped onto the elevated deck and stood beside Moses and Cyrus. He faced the seated elders and said, "First, we appeared before Pharaoh as the leadership of a foreign nation opposing his reign here in Egypt. Secondly, we challenged his sovereignty by delivering a demand from a God he does not recognize. We should have gone in humbly and petitioned the Pharaoh for some time away from our duties so that we could observe a religious festival. Instead, we challenged him, almost dared him to deny our demand, and in so doing alerted him to our desire to leave Egypt. Now, to confirm his hold on us, he will make our task more difficult and increase the hours we labor, and have his guards watch us closer.

Are we now to say, *'well done, Moses*?' And tell me, Cyrus, will you stand before our people and encourage them to bear the increased workload and harshness brought on by our challenge to Pharaoh?"

Moses laid a hand on Zevs' shoulder and said, "This young man well illustrates the questions our people will put to us. He has made their argument for them, and in answer, we must tell the people to be patient, and in the fullness of time, when God has shown that he and he alone rules in the affairs of men and nations, we will leave Egypt. Tell them to believe and to begin preparing for the journey by storing provision and by secreting away as much treasure as possible, for God has said that we will not leave Egypt destitute."

Zev shrugged his shoulders, and said, "And where will you and Aaron be while we are telling our people to bear the burden and believe in our future deliverance?"

Moses placed his hands in Zevs' and said, "We will be bearing the burden with them. Tell them that, and then tell them to watch as God brings judgment after judgment on Pharaoh, remind them that as each day passes, the day of our deliverance comes closer. Finally, tell them that for now we wait."

Chapter Twenty-Seven
Ramses Reacts

Ramses watched Moses, and the Elders leave the chamber. "Captain, did you tell me they arrived by boat?"

"Yes, highness."

"Watch them board; Count them so we can be sure they all have left the palace grounds. Be sure Moses is on the boat, then report to me."

"Yes, highness."

Ramses sat silently until the captain returned to say Moses and the elders were gone. "Good. Members I want you to pay attention to what I say. Scribes take care to record what I am about to order."

"Captain, you will gather the taskmasters. Tell them that I order that they no longer give straw to the Hebrews to make bricks. It is my order that the Hebrews gather straw for themselves. Furthermore, the quota of bricks they are to make will remain unchanged. They are to have no idle time, work them from sun rise to sun set, lay more work on them than ever before. Tell the overseers that they are to hold the Hebrews who they have set as officers over the laborers accountable. Lay the lash on the officers when the slaves fail to meet their quotas."

Ramses looked to the court members and said, "I do not need your approval, but for the record, you may speak in support, or in opposition, or you may ask me any question you have about my decision."

Ramen glanced at the other members and then said, "Thank you, Pharaoh, for asking our opinion. As I see it, this is the rebellion your father feared. To appear before you and make any demand is unthinkable, but to demand that you allow them to leave your presence, to worship this Hebrew God is nothing other than a declaration of independence. They forget that they are a captive people. Liberty, in Egypt, is yours to give in any measure you choose. Your Highness has two choices, free them and remove them from Egypt, or tighten their chains, increasing their bondage until they surrender to your sovereign reign over them."

"Well said, Ramen. And which of these options do you recommend?"

"Your majesty should expel them from Egypt. In doing so, you will not have surrendered to their demand; you will have asserted your sovereignty and exercised your power, saying they are no longer welcome in your Kingdom and by driving them out."

"Hmmm, interesting idea, Ramen. But why would I throw away, expel if you will, such an asset? Do you not agree that we have profited greatly from the labor of the Hebrews?"

"We have indeed, majesty, but we have reached a point where we no longer profit from them. The exponential increase in their numbers, is requiring more and more resources to manage and control them; thus, moving them from asset to liability. The enemies outside our borders are threat enough, why should we allow the continued increase of this internal threat. Expelling them removes that threat."

Ramses thought a minute and said, "Thank you Ramen, I am confident the other members from your generation will agree with you; What about you younger members? Zephyr, I choose you to speak for them. Is Ramen, right? Should we expel them?"

"Only if your majesty wants to yield to them. All Ramen's suggestion does is put a different spin on their demands. The 'expulsion' will be seen as a surrender to the demands and threats of the Hebrews. It will weaken us in the eyes of those external enemies Ramen spoke of. So no, the prudent thing to do is to tighten their chains, increase their burden and force them to yield to the greater power of Pharaoh's hand."

Ramses nodded, then said to Ramen, "I will give you the last word out of respect to your service to my father. What do you expect if I follow Zephyr's counsel?"

"This is what I expect, majesty. The Hebrews will not be able to meet their quotas given the new requirement to gather their own straw. The overseers will lay the lash on their officers as you have ordered. Their officers will complain to Moses, Moses, and Aaron will return to you and renew their request for you to let them go. You will refuse and curse their cause. The conflict will escalate; they have tasted the hope of liberty, they will not submit. Your cursing of them will bring a curse on Egypt collectively and you individually. There is an aura of power, some mystical presence in this man Moses. My spirit tells me that he commands more than a people; he has a connection to the source of this power and will wield it against us. Let them go, majesty."

Ramses laughed and replied, "I don't believe in the mystical. My Decision stands. It has been written; now let it be done."

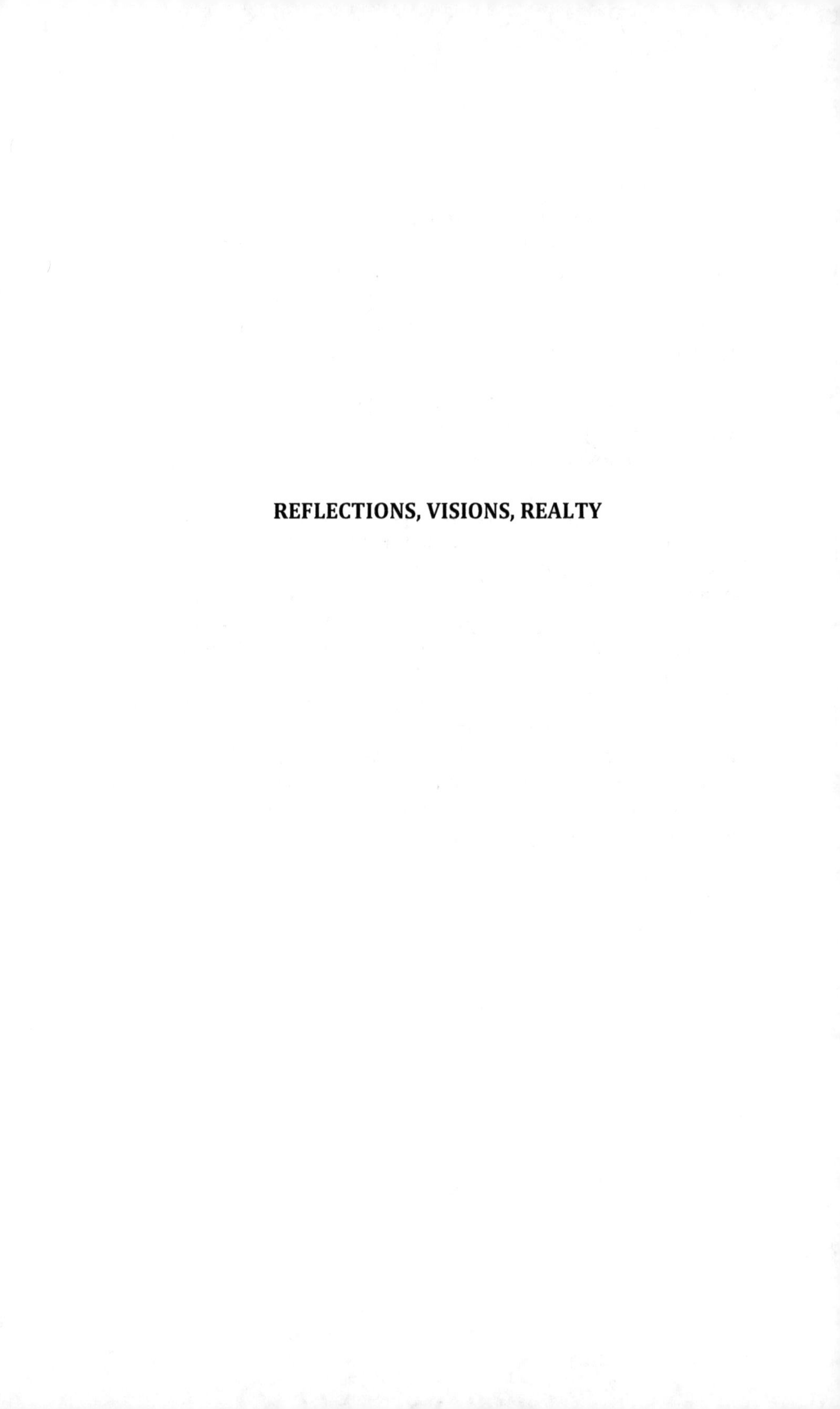

REFLECTIONS, VISIONS, REALTY

Chapter Twenty-Eight

The Decision

Moses sat in the shade of an outcropping of rock at the base of Mount Nebo. A lively breeze whistled its' way through the narrow passage. Moses shifted so the breeze could pass under the hem of his robe, soothing his aching legs. On impulse, he pulled the hem up past his knees so he could see his upper legs. He grimaced at the sight, '*sagging wrinkles and yellowing flesh. Still, they work, and that is good for a hundred- and twenty-year-old man. The question is, will they carry me to the top of God's Mountain? I am going to say yes because He commanded me to climb it. I believe these old legs would take me across the Jordan, but then that Decision has been made.'*

He pushed the robe down and leaned back against the rock wall remembering his last conversation with his Lord, *'O Lord God, you have begun to show Your servant Your greatness and Your mighty hand, for what God is there in heaven or on earth who can do anything like Your works and Your mighty deeds?*

I pray, let me cross over and see the good land beyond the Jordan, those pleasant mountains, and Lebanon.

Moses winced, remembering how the Lord had grown angry, and said, "Enough of that! Speak no more to me of this matter. Go to the top of Nebo and lift your eyes toward the west, the north, the south, and the east; behold the land that I promised to the descendants of Abraham. You may see it, but you will not be allowed to cross the Jordan. I have spoken.

You are to command Joshua and encourage him and strengthen him; for he shall go over before this people, and he shall cause them to inherit the land which you will see."

The Decision was made, and Moses knew it was a final decision. So, he sat here, at the foot of Mount Nebo, ready to obey his Lord's command. He vowed that he would follow the Lord's instruction to the letter, *'If only I had done so with the rock. I would be preparing to lead my people into their promised land,'* he thought. Moses moved out of the shadows and started the climb.

The sky was clear of clouds, and the sun poured its' unhindered heat down on Moses. The slopes were covered with loose stones. They worked their way into his sandals and were a torture to his bare feet.

Moses stumbled and started to slide backward, down the steep slope. He was able to stop his descent by wrapping his arms around a flat-topped boulder. The momentum of his downward slide pulled the muscles in his shoulders and upper arms. Moses felt his strength ebbing and knew that he was close to a free fall down the Mountain. With the last of his power, he pulled himself even with the flat-topped stone and sat on it.

A spasm worked its way through his lower back, running alongside his spine to his shoulders. The pain raced across his shoulders up the back of his neck and down into his upper arms. He sat captive to the spasm. His eyes watered in response to the pain. Moses leaned forward, resting his elbows on his knees. His robe stretched tight across his back and shoulders. With his back exposed to the sun, The heat that had taken his vitality now became his healer, the spasms stopped as his muscles absorbed the warmth and relaxed under its' soothing caress.

Moses shifted forward and eased down the face of the stone, leaning his aching back against its' warm surface. He removed his sandals and shook the rocks from them. His feet were bleeding. He pulled the scarf from around his neck, tore it in half, and wrapped his feet.

Moses stretched his legs and allowed the sun to heat and soothe his feet. He lay the back of his head against the stones' smooth surface and looked to the top of the Mountain. He had started the climb early this morning. He had been sure that he could make it. Now he sat here less than halfway up the slope and wondered if he had enough left in him to reach the top.

As he pondered the climb, Moses heard in his spirit, *'Rest here until the heat of the day is gone, and then move up as far as you can in the evening's fading light. I have prepared a bed of gravel where you can sleep. Rest there and then push to the summit tomorrow morning before the sun heats the air.'*

Satisfied with this plan, Moses yielded to his exhaustion and slept. His body rested, but his mind did not. He dreamed and was once more a boy, running through the palace, playing hide and seek with Ramses and the other children of royalty. Moses was unaware of the smile that these memories brought to his face as he slept.

Nor was he aware of the frown and the grinding of his teeth that came as his dream shifted from carefree childhood to his maturation and realization that he was born a Hebrew. The dream was often repeated, and as always, Moses woke at the point of his killing the Egyptian.

The sun had started its downward march in the Western sky, and long shadows now surrounded the boulder against which Moses rested. He stood and looked to the top of the Mountain, measuring the distance he had yet to travel, *'I have three hours before darkness will make it too dangerous to climb. By that time, I will be within a mile of the summit. I will sleep through the night and start my climb again at first light. I will be in place to watch the crossing by mid-afternoon,'* Moses reasoned.

He took one last look at the setting sun and then started his climb. The cool air refreshed Moses, and he made good time. Three hours later, he came to a pond of loose gravel created by a past landslide. The little area was surrounded by a wall of waist-high boulders. *'My resting place that the Lord has prepared for me. The gravel will be my bed, and the boulders will keep the wind off me,'* Moses thought as he removed his sandals, pulled his robes close about his body, and stretched out on his back.

Moses stared at the stars, *'what a magnificent covering the Creator has given the earth! I wonder is it a covering for the earth or is it the flooring for heaven?' 'Lord, I have so many questions, can I ask them now?'* Moses did not hear an answer, but he reasoned, *'since You did not say no I am going to just ask my questions, so here we go Lord.'* "Lord, did you know I was going to kill that Egyptian? If you did, why didn't you change the events so I would not kill him? Lord you must have known that Ramses would refuse to let us go, so why did you send Aaron and me into his court to ask it? Why Lord, when you could have prevented the plagues, the suffering, the death of the first born. I believe that You knew each one, that you gave life to each one, so why not change events so those lives were not forfeit to that which you knew was going to happen? Why did you part the sea and give us safe passage, but closed it in over the Egyptians, was there not another way without all that loss of life? You made such wonderful provision for us in the wilderness, food when we were hungry, water when we were thirsty, yet you kept us there for forty years walking in circles on what should have been a three day walk, why not just deliver us from the wilderness into the promised land? Why did an entire generation have to perish? Lord you knew I was going to strike that rock and in doing so lose my opportunity to lead these people across the Jordan. Why did You not stop me, why did you take me this far and now deny me the crossing? I just don't understand Lord, do you have an answer for me?"

"Moses, Moses, Moses! Yes, I have more answers than your finite mind can handle. For now, try to understand this; I created everything that is, and all of it is there for me, for my glory. And in the end, all of creation, will glorify me. Mankind I created in my image and likeness because I desired fellowship with them. I could have commanded that fellowship but what I wanted was for mankind to come to me because they wanted to come to me. Therefore, I instilled free will in all mankind, and that includes you, Moses. Yes, I could have changed events to cause Pharoah to allow my people to leave the bondage he imposed on them, and yes, I could have prevented your killing of the Egyptian, and yes, I could have prevented you from striking the stone. But that is not my way. Try to understand this Moses, my sovereign will flows concurrently with your free choices. Your free will then determines how events in your life play out. I gave you numerous notices that your intemperate passions would lead to you not fulfilling your destiny, but you ignored each notice. You alone are responsible for your actions and the consequences thereof. Still, I know your heart and my grace is sufficient for your redemption You will see me in all my glory and your tongue will sing of that glory in its' eternity. Now rest, you have a climb to finish tomorrow."

Moses was lifted from the deep sleep of exhaustion by a sharp pain in his foot. He sat up and saw a crow roosting on his lower leg pecking at the dried blood on his foot.

Moses swatted the bird. It flew away but settled on a rock not far from where Moses lay. The bird flapped his wings and scolded Moses for disturbing his breakfast. Moses gathered a handful of the loose gravel and cast it at the bird. The bird hopped out of the way, caught an updraft and began airborne surveillance of Moses, circling overhead as if unwilling to give up on his breakfast.

Disgusted, Moses wished for water with which he could wash his feet and slake his thirst, but he had downed the last of his meager supply with his food the night before. The thought of food made him aware of how hungry he was this morning.

He realized he had been short-sighted in not bringing enough provision for the climb: *'ten years ago I could have made it to the summit in one day, but ten years ago I was a young man of one hundred and ten years,'* Moses laughed at himself.

Moses knew that his time of service in the Exodus of Israel from slavery was at an end. Moses accepted the Lords' Decision and kneeled before the Lord in worship, saying, "Thank you, Lord. You preserved my life as a babe set adrift in a basket on the Nile, you provided my birth mother to be present so I would feed on the milk of my ancestors, you positioned and prepared me for leadership as a Prince of Egypt. You confirmed me as an heir of the Abrahamic Covent by allowing me to lead my brethren in this Exodus. You parted the Red Sea so we could escape Pharaoh on dry land and then closed the waters in over the horse and rider who pursued us. You fed us in the wilderness; you provided water in the desert; you gave us the law and then forgave us when we abandoned it. You preserved me when the people rebelled against my leadership, and you sustained me in my weakness. Great is Thy faithfulness.

You have graciously given me one hundred and twenty years of life. You have decided my time here in this dispensation is ending. Yet again, you are showing your generosity by sending me to the top of this Mountain that I might see the promised land.

I am going to obey your command and climb to the Pisgah; I humbly ask that you allow me time and grant me the ability to reflect on the past as I see the promised land. Grant me this, my Lord, I pray."

Moses rose from prayer and started his climb. His nights' sleep had restored his strength, and he stepped out with vigor. The fast pace drained Moses' strength: and he found himself stumbling as the lack of food and water took its' toll on him.

His vision blurred, and he gasped for breath. Through a roaring in his head, he heard a mocking voice say, "*You are finished, a used-up old man, the Lord has withdrawn his hand from you because of your disobedience in striking the rock rather than calling it forth in his name that the people might know that he was with them as he had been at the parting of the Red Sea and the provision of manna. You have lived long, and you have lived well, but you had also fulfilled the prophecy of Ramses when he said that you would fail to fulfill your destiny because of your propensity to do things your way rather than as it had been ordered.*

You have forfeited the privilege of leading Israel into Canaan. I now have a license to contend for your soul. Your flesh will rot, and your bones will turn to dust here on this Mountain, but your soul will live, and I aim to contend for it."

Moses had heard this voice many times; he heard it as he killed the Egyptian, he heard it as he fled into Midian, he heard it in the voice of his wife when she urged him not to circumcise their son, he heard it laughing when God sought to kill him in the camp as he returned to Egypt. But Moses remembered that at such times there was always another voice, the voice from the flame in the bush, the voice that guided him in the military training and exercises as a member of the royal family, and the voice declaring the plagues in Egypt if Pharaoh refused to let the Israelites go.

Moses looked to the heavens and said, "Speak to me, Lord. I have heard the voice of the enemy; I need to hear your voice. Arise my Lord and scatter the enemy of your servant; I accept your Decision; my time has run, and I am ready. I ask that you deny the enemy in his claim for my soul. Forgive your servant wherein I have failed you; remember my service to you, I pray. Allow your servant to be witness to the deliverance of Israel and then draw me to your side."

Chapter Twenty-Nine

The Crossing

Moses finished his prayer and struggled to his feet. His knees locked on him as he tried to stand, and he fell forward. Instinct caused him to thrust his hands to break his fall. The sharp-edged rocks cut into his palms. His forearms gave way, and he crashed face-first into the rock-strew ground. An involuntary cry escaped his cracked lips, and Moses heard the laughing voice of his enemy. A shadow passed over him, and Moses looked to the sky; hovering there, riding a thermal updraft, was the crow. The voice spoke again, "*He knows that you are dying Moses; he will ride the winds and wait. He will have your flesh. I will have your soul.*"

Blood trickled down his forehead and dropped onto his lips. Moses' tongue darted out to capture the blood; he licked it from his lips and drew it into his parched mouth. He swallowed; as soon as the blood left his mouth to slide down his throat, Moses felt a rush of energy. His vision cleared. His legs pulsed with strength, and Moses stood tall and steady. He heard a gasp from his enemy. Moses laughed, "You were saying?

"Look at me now! I am standing strong, and my vision is not diminished. I can hear the people gathering along the bank of the Jordan, eleven thousand feet below, in preparation for the crossing. There is Joshua's voice; I can hear it above the din of those who are pushing, wanting to cross. He is telling them to wait, the Jordan is at flood stage, and the current is too strong. He is holding them until the flood subsides, and that gives me time to reach the peak."

Moses felt a hand on his back, pushing him forward. He looked over his shoulder and heard, "Don't look back; that which is behind you is of no consequence. Instead, look forward, go to the peak, and I will grant your request and allow you the time for reflection, but Moses, you will not see the crossing. But, I promise you will be more pleased with that which you will see. For, today you will see my glory."

Moses yielded to the pressure on his back and strode to the peak of the Mountain. The air was cool, the skies were clear, and Moses could see the people preparing to cross over into the promised land. Moses looked closely at the flooding river, and suddenly he knew, *'The Lord will impose his sovereign will over the natural in favor of his people Israel, and they will cross safely into their inheritance.'*

Moses stood on the windswept peak and saw Joshua retreat from the Jordan; He watched as Joshua spread his hands in exasperation. Then Joshua turned back to stand on the bank of the Jordan.

Moses heard him shout to the people, "Make camp here. We will wait until the flood subsides, and then we will cross."

Moses nodded in agreement and asked, "How long yet, Lord? This river marks the end of their wilderness experience. Why hold them back? Let them cross now."

"Moses, Moses, there you go again, letting your passion lead you. Forty years they have been in the wilderness. They stand now on the brink of being set free. But I will require three days to give them time to understand that I AM. I alone rule in the affairs of men, nations, and nature is mine to command.

CHAPTER Thirty

Pisgah Perch

Moses recognized the tone. He searched for a place to sit and reflect on the past as he accepted the present and looked forward to the future. There was an ageless boulder near the edge of the summit. The sun was now behind him, and the stone cast a shadow that reached to the edge and dropped down the face of the mountain. Moses placed on hand on the rough rim of the boulder, tested his grip, and wiggled himself around in front. He looked down and shivered as he realized he was three feet from a drop into the valley below. The voice spoke, "*Go ahead, take charge, say when your life will end. One step into space and you will be pain-free, and if you believe your God, He will bear you up, and you will see that glory he spoke of, in fact you will spend eternity in it with him.'*

Moses replied, "Did you not hear him? He is the I AM; He and He alone rules in the affairs of men. He wrote my life, the days, and the events. He and He alone will end those days."

Moses heard a flapping noise and glanced back to see the crow had landed on the boulder and was watching him. Moses lifted his hand to shoo the bird away and, in doing so, felt himself slip toward the edge. The voice laughed, and Moses realized he was being baited. He said, "Satan, I will recognize you no more. You can struggle with God, but then you have tried that once and lost, you will lose again."

Moses faced forward-looking into the cloudless sky, the wind whipping up the face of the Mountain passed over him in the shade and soothed his aching legs. Moses pulled the sandals from his feet and tossed them over the edge. *'I will not need them again,'* he thought. He stretched his legs, his bare feet, forward, dangling over the side of the Mountain. The calming cool soon had him sleeping, he leaned back against a foundation stone, with his feet hanging over the edge of Nebo in his Pisgah perch.

CHAPTER Thirty-One

THE ROCK

As Moses slept, his body relaxed, his mind opened, and he heard his father's voice, *'It is time Jochebed; we cannot hide him forever. We must let him go.'* His mother cried, *'My beautiful child.'* He saw his mother remove the basket from behind the stone hearth, felt her tears fall on his face as she lay him in the basket, saw Miriam's face as she leaned over and kissed him, he saw his mother's face as she lowered him into the Nile and pushed him away from her. He was afloat, bouncing and rocking on the waves. The basket floated in amongst the reeds, and he heard a shout, *'Look, it is a basket, bring it to me.'* Moses remembered the brown face looking down at him; he remembered the kind eyes, the smile, and her gentle hands as he was lifted from the basket. The next thing he remembered was being handed back to his mother, her soft breast and the comfort of the warm milk flooding his mouth as he suckled.

Then he was sitting on Seti's knee, reaching for his crown, and dropping it on the table next to a candle. He saw Ramses, and his heart was heavy as he remembered Ramses telling him they were not brothers. He remembered the powerful feeling of knowing who he was. He remembered when he resolved to protect his people, the pain of their initial rejection of him, shame washed over him as the scene of his murdering the Egyptian came up before him. Moses squirmed on the ledge, remembering his frantic efforts to bury the dead man in the dune. His squirming caused some loose stones to cascade over the edge. Moses anchored himself by pushing his hands into the rocky soil, reminding himself to respect his precious perch. *'Here I sit on the edge of the mountain of God, hanging between what is left of this life and the beginning of the next.'* Moses mused.

The voice spoke, "*So why not push forward into the void and fall into your future, but the pain and rebuke of not being able to lead your people into their future behind you. Just push off; he will end it for you before you hit the ground.*"

Moses grinned, "So you admit that it is His to determine when a man lives and when he dies?" He heard a rustle; then, the breeze bathed the right side of his face. *'He was there, in front of me, ready and waiting, tempting me to defy the sovereignty of God by ending the life He gave me.'* Moses mulled this over and then leaned his head back against the rock and shouted into the darkening sky, "Satan, I know you have departed; waiting for another opportunity to wage war against me as you do with all the sons of the woman. Just know this, there is no void for those who walk with him, and my choice has been and is to walk with him. if I fall, He will be there to catch me."

Moses heard a shuffle and braced himself, fearing the enemy would try to push him over the edge. There was a stillness, a peace, the whistling of the wind ceased. For Moses it was more than a change, he felt a transition. He looked to his bare legs and feet, the wrinkled sagging flesh was gone and there were the legs and feet of his youth. He looked at his hands and arms to see the same transition. There was a soft caress on his shoulders; Moses felt himself being lifted but his body remained seated. He glanced down as he was lifted away from the edge. Moses knew he was in the hands of God. He relaxed as God settled him on the rock that had braced his back. God spoke to him as he had on Mount Sinai, "Moses, Moses, you have asked for a time to reflect on your life, do you remember when I said this to you? *'There is a place near Me where you are to stand upon a rock, and when My glory passes by, I will put you in a cleft of the rock and cover you with My hand until I have passed. Then I will take My hand away, and you will see My back, but My face must not be seen.* 'The cleft was necessary because my presence would have pushed you from the Mountain; I had to cover your face because no man can see my face and continue to live. That was then but now there is no cleft in the rock on which you stand. I am standing beside you; I am not passing you by.

You may now look full on my face, for you are no longer a man; you are now a spirit. The purpose for which I created you is complete. Your flesh shall remain here on my Mountain, but you are now with me. Your spirit has returned from whence it came."

Moses was lifted away from the rock and into the night. He glanced down and looked to the river trying to see the people crossing but there was a cloud blocking his vision. He looked to the rock on which he had stood. His body was not there. He asked himself, *'Where is my body,'* and he heard, 'Hush Moses, the rock has stood there through the ages, waiting for this time. It will continue to stand until I end all time. Many will come searching the rock for your remains, but they will find nothing because there are no remains. You are alive and together with me. You are now in my glory.

Moses looked up to find that he was among the stars. They were singing. Their singing wrapped him in a soft warmth. He saw the dark skies turn to glistening milky glow. He felt a presence that he could not identify, a peace penetrated and filled him and then beside him were figures in white. They were not leading him as much as escorting him. All around him was the sound of unknown tongues. He asked his escort what the singers were saying, they pointed for him to look ahead and as he did, he saw a city of light. He felt their answer, you will know as we enter, and as he passed through the gates the tongues became clear. Without a conscious effort he found himself joining them in their song, *'Holy, Holy, Holy is the Lord God Almighty, Who was, Who is and Who is to come.'* "Holy, Holy, Holy is the Lord God Almighty, who was, who is, and who is to come. Moses was home.

The Beginning…

AMEN

MOSES WAVING GOODBYE AS HE DEPARTS MOUNT NEBO
From old bible story books
Courtesy of La Vistia Church of Christ
HTTP://LAVISTIACHURCHOFCHRIST.ORG

PUBLIC DOMAIN

AFTER GLOW~

Moses was witness to and agent of many supernatural events in his life, but he was a natural man. He was invested with the spirit of He who created him. Like all investors his creator expected a return. Moses returned the investment with a great profit (no pun intended). He stumbled, he failed, but he was judged by the content of his heart. When his time had run, he who had sent him came to take him home. I like to believe that as Moses ascended, he was met and accompanied by Angels in white, escorting him home to the city of love wherein he lives today singing the praise of our lord. I like to think that is how it will be for me, you, for all of us who stand on the ROCK. This will be our story on that day:

<u>City of Love, River of Praise</u>

The day began as all I had known
Time with the Lord just after dawn

The day progressed as had the last
Then came the horn's blast

All things changed in the twinkle of an eye
No longer on the earth I was flying through the sky

Peace I felt surrounded by light
Flying beside me were Angels in white

Up ahead a city like none where I had been
The gates stood open; and we flew in

A City of Love with a River of Praise
I knew that herein reigned the Ancient of Days

The gates were of pearl, the streets of gold
Just as our fathers had foretold

People all around me I was not alone
We were ushered before the master's throne

Thereon a Presence with glory and power
Beside Him a Lamb; as if slain within the hour

Every knee did bow, every tongue did sing
It is true O Lord; You are the King of Kings

The Book was opened, my name was found
It was written there, in the Blood of the Lamb

His face turns, His eyes I see
Love flowed forth, penetrating me

He speaks with a roar, a sound like the wind
Well done; come in My friend

Oh, what joy now fills my days
Always in His presence, singing His praise

It is not what I did but Whom I knew
Thank you, Lord, I am here because of You

ABOUT THE AUTHOR

~

Ken Bangs

A native Texan, Ken was born in Cooper, Delta County, and raised in Plano, Collin County. Ken is a veteran of the United States Army. Ken spent his life in law enforcement and public safety. He earned a B.S. in criminal justice from Sam Houston State University, a M.S. in Human Relations and Business Management from Amber University and a Doctor of Ministry, in counseling from Jacksonville, Florida, theological seminary.

Ken is married to Trudy Turner Bangs. They celebrated 53 years of marriage in 2021. They have two children, Kristen, and Ken. They also have two ***perfect*** grandchildren, Miranda, and Kenneth W. Bangs, III.

Trudy and Ken live in McKinney, Texas.

OTHER BOOKS BY KEN BANGS

Rosco Jack of Gateway Farm & The return of the Pirate

Arctic Warriors

Guardians in Blue

Guardians in Blue (book two)

The Levy

Out of Saul ~ Paul

Coming Next

Once a Wildcat

First to Fall

By His Blood We Are Healed ~ because of His cross we live

Daniel

www.ingramcontent.com/pod-product-compliance
Lightning Source LLC
LaVergne TN
LVHW050535100826
845148LV00002B/572

* 9 7 8 1 7 3 3 1 1 9 4 7 4 *